TRUTHFORLIFE®

THE BIBLE-TEACHING MINISTRY OF **ALISTAIR BEGG**

The mission of Truth For Life is to teach the Bible with clarity and relevance so that unbelievers will be converted, believers will be established, and local churches will be strengthened.

Daily Program

Each day, Truth For Life distributes the Bible teaching of Alistair Begg across the U.S. and in several locations outside of the U.S. through 1,800 radio outlets. To find a radio station near you, visit **truthforlife.org/stationfinder**.

Free Teaching

The daily program, and Truth For Life's entire teaching archive of over 2,000 Bible-teaching messages, can be accessed for free online and through Truth For Life's full-feature mobile app. Download the free mobile app at **truthforlife.org/app** and listen free online at **truthforlife.org**.

At-Cost Resources

Books and full-length teaching from Alistair Begg on CD, DVD, and USB are available for purchase at cost, with no markup. Visit **truthforlife.org/store**.

Where to Begin?

If you're new to Truth For Life and would like to know where to begin listening and learning, find starting point suggestions at **truthforlife.org/firststep**. For a full list of ways to connect with Truth For Life, visit **truthforlife.org/subscribe**.

Contact Truth For Life

P.O. Box 398000 Cleveland, Ohio 44139
phone 1 (888) 588-7884   **email** letters@truthforlife.org
 /truthforlife   @truthforlife   truthforlife.org

"It's overwhelming to think of all the things I'd like to tell someone who is starting their journey of following Christ. I'm so glad Gary Millar wrote this book; he distills and explains what you need to know in a way that anyone can understand. This book is clear, faithful and relatable, and will be a joy to start giving away to friends!"

GLORIA FURMAN, Author, *Treasuring Christ When Your Hands Are Full* and *Labor with Hope*

"I thoroughly enjoyed this book. Gary Millar has given us that rare combination: an accessible book written in a warm, engaging, realistic style but with content that has a depth arising from a thorough and thoughtful biblical and theological understanding. It will be a thoroughly useful book, and I commend it warmly."

CHRISTOPHER ASH, Writer-in-Residence, Tyndale House, Cambridge

"Because more and more people who come to genuine faith in Christ have little or no Christian background, it is becoming more and more important to orientate them to Christian life and thought. What is needed is something of a cross between a gentle introduction to basic Christian belief and a 'how-to' manual. This book is it."

D. A. CARSON, Research Professor, Trinity Evangelical Divinity School

"Gary Millar may be trained as an Old Testament scholar, but he has always had an eye on the practical questions, concerns and needs of ordinary Christians. In this book, he does what he is most passionate about: explaining and applying the basic principles of the Christian faith in an accessible and attractive manner. This little book is as edifying as it is entertaining."

CARL R. TRUEMAN, Professor of Biblical and Religious Studies, Grove City College

"This book tells you what you need to know to live the Christian life, and it does it with clarity, honesty, realism, humour and graciousness. Millar's style is very practical and down to earth. We're left with a real sense of both the privilege and the responsibility it is to live for Jesus, and a clear idea of what this will look like in everyday life."

JANE TOOHER, Lecturer, Moore College

"This is a concisely comprehensive little book. It provides so much for so many different kinds of people. Enlightenment for the suspicious. Challenge for the complacent. Guidance for the seeking. Instruction for the questioning. Refreshment for the forgetful (people like me). Gary not only tells but shows how the gospel is for everyone... and how anyone can take their next step forward."

JOHN ONWUCHEKWA, Lead Pastor, Cornerstone Church, Atlanta

"If there is one profound yet simple book to read that will help you watch your life and doctrine closely, this is it. Gary Millar has written an engaging, Bible-saturated and Christ-exalting guide to the gospel-shaped life, which he clearly lives."

RICHARD CHIN, National Director, The Australian Fellowship of Evangelical Students; Author, *Captivated by Christ*

"You were made to know and enjoy God. This book may be short and seemingly simple, but it will point you in the direction of solid and serious joy that begins now and lasts forever. Short doesn't mean trivial. This book addresses the most important quest in the universe, and Gary Millar is a good guide."

DAVID MATHIS, Senior Teacher and Executive Editor, desiringGod.org; Pastor, Cities Church, Minneapolis, Minnesota; Author, *Habits of Grace: Enjoying Jesus Through the Spiritual Disciplines*

Need to Know
© 2020 Gary Millar

This edition printed in partnership
with *Truth For Life*, 2020

Published by:
The Good Book Company

thegoodbook.com | www.thegoodbook.co.uk
thegoodbook.com.au | thegoodbook.co.nz | thegoodbook.co.in

ISBN: 9781784984427 | Printed in the UK

Design by André Parker

CONTENTS

INTRODUCTION

———

I have a love-hate relationship with flatpack furniture.

I love it when I'm looking at it online or in the store. As I browse the stylishly designed, ingeniously practical and (here's the important one) *fully assembled* furniture, I grow more and more excited at the idea of having it in my home. The small print assures me that no expertise (or co-ordination) is needed to put it together. So I say to myself, "This time will be different!" and part with my hard-earned cash.

Then I get my new purchase home and open the box. What I thought would be straightforward now seems overwhelming...

As I unpack the carton, there are so many nuts and bolts, wood-veneer panels, and bits and pieces of plastic that my head starts to spin. It's confusing. It's overwhelming. And inevitably, I do something wrong. Over the years I have managed to put the top on the bottom, the front on the back and everything else upside down. I have lost pieces, sheared screws and accidentally snapped vital components. This catalogue of disasters often unfolds to the soundtrack of members of my family offering "helpful" advice or pointing out what has gone wrong.

The really annoying thing is that every time, my mistakes could have been avoided if I had just taken five minutes at the start to read through the instruction sheet. It would have told me everything I needed to know. I may not be a practical person, but I can read. The trouble is that I prefer to just rush into things, and then act surprised (and get frustrated) when stuff inevitably goes wrong. I would have saved myself so much time (and pain) if I'd slowed down right at the start to think through the basic steps I needed to take.

Living as a Christian can sometimes feel a little like assembling flatpack furniture. Maybe you're at the overwhelming, just-got-everything-out-of-the-box stage. You signed yourself up for this Christian thing on the basis of the picture in the catalogue—but now you're not quite sure which bit goes where, or what to do next (and there are *lots* of weird words for things). Or maybe you've been a Christian for a while, but you're starting to wonder whether it's meant to look like this (especially as when you peer through the windows of other Christians' lives, their flatpack furniture seems to be in a far better state than yours).

Much like assembling flatpack furniture, when it comes to living for Jesus, there are some basic principles and key steps that we need to take (and keep taking) if we are to pull it off. The great news is that not only has God spelled out for us really clearly in the Bible what life with him involves, but he has also given us his Holy Spirit to help us live for and with him. (I'll explain all that in the chapters that follow.)

This book is intended to set you up for living for Jesus with the whole of your life for the rest of your life. In this book, we'll call this living the "gospel-shaped" life—one that is completely moulded around the good news about Jesus.

I've tried to make this book really clear and simple (but more interesting than an instruction manual!). I've also tried to keep it short. Whether you are a new Christian or have been one for a while and feel in need of a refresher, or have been around church for years but are finding things have only just clicked into place for you, I hope you'll find it helpful. It doesn't even begin to try to say everything that could be said about the Christian life, but it should give you the essentials—what you really need to know if you're going to follow Jesus.

I do hope that this book will whet your appetite to read more and more about what it means to live for Christ. For almost 2,000 years, some of the greatest minds in history have poured their energies into writing about God and what he asks of us. In the few pages that follow, I have tried to distil what they have said into just over a hundred pages of fairly large type. It's very much a broad-brush introduction which assumes you'll then want to look more closely at the details for the rest of your life. But hopefully, as you do, you'll realise that even though the details come into sharper focus the longer we go on in our faith, the big picture itself—the shape of the Christian life—doesn't change.

There is one key difference between putting together a bookcase or a coffee table (or even a rocking chair—my finest achievement to date!) and living as a Christian. Even though it may take a while (and a few mis-steps) to assemble flatpack furniture, eventually the job is done, and we can stand back and admire our handiwork. But living a gospel-shaped life is a "project" that we never finish in this life—we'll never feel that we've "made it" as a Christian. It's an exciting lifetime project of changing and growing and being transformed, bit by bit, to be like Jesus—until God finishes the work in eternity.

And that's why this book is worth reading. Because there really is nothing better than that.

1. KNOWING THE GOD
OF THE GOSPEL

"Now this is eternal life: that they know you, the only
true God, and Jesus Christ, whom you have sent."
(John 17 v 3)

It's always hard to resist listening in on other people's conversations.

A couple of years ago, I happened to be having breakfast with an astronaut (as you do). Colonel Jeff Williams had spent a total of 564 days in space, so over breakfast I asked him all the questions that I have wanted to ask an astronaut since I was a kid. Are you scared when you're basically strapped to a giant bomb ready for lift-off? What is it like looking out at space when you're on a space walk? How's the food? When we started to talk, it was just us in the quiet hotel breakfast room. About 45 minutes later, I realised that the room had filled up, but *nobody else was saying anything*. One by one, they had come in, heard Jeff mention NASA or the International Space Station, and just started listening to our conversation. I would have done the same! Listening in on an astronaut is fascinating.

John 17 is one of the most remarkable chapters in the whole Bible for this reason. It comes at the end of a section of John's Gospel which gives us a detailed account of the final things Jesus said to his disciples on the night before he died (chapters 13 – 17). Chapter 17 gives us the opportunity to listen in not on an astronaut but the living God, as Jesus prays to his Father in heaven.

Now that's pretty astounding in itself—this is God's "private conversation", as God the Son talks to God the Father. But it's what Jesus actually *prays for* that's even more remarkable.

Here's how the conversation starts:

[1] Jesus ... looked towards heaven and prayed: "Father, the hour has come. Glorify your Son, that your Son may glorify you. [2] For you granted him authority over all people that he might give eternal life to all those you have given him. [3] Now this is eternal life: that they know you, the only true God, and Jesus Christ, whom you have sent. [4] I have brought you glory on earth by finishing the work you gave me to do. [5] And now, Father, glorify me in your presence with the glory I had with you before the world began."

This whole scene is very intense. The "hour" that has come is for Jesus' death (v 1).

So on the last night of his life, what's Jesus thinking about? He is thinking about us. Jesus is about to do the unimaginable—he is about to die for people like you and me. He's about to step in to face the punishment that we earned and to face the Father's anger which we had provoked. He is going through with this so that he can give people like us an unparalleled gift—*eternal life*: "For you granted [your Son] authority over all people that he might give eternal life to all those you have given him" (v 2).

Eternal life. Generally in the Bible that means *life with God that starts now and goes on for ever.* But here Jesus gives us an even simpler definition of this life than that—he calls it *knowing God*: "Now this is eternal life: that they know you, the only true God, and Jesus Christ, whom you have sent" (v 3). To be a Christian—to have eternal life—is to know God. We don't often think of it like this, but *knowing God* is the very heart of the Christian life.

So I hope you've got this: Jesus Christ, the Lord of all, within 24 hours of his excruciating death, as he prepares to bear the full weight of the sins of the world, is preoccupied with one thing. He's preoccupied with us—and in particular, with our life.

What does Jesus want for you? *Jesus wants you to know God.* That's because at its heart, Christianity isn't really about us—it's about God. It's important to get that straight (and it makes the whole "living for Jesus" thing much, much easier!). That's why this first chapter is all about God—and, more specifically, about *knowing God.*

So what does that involve? Two things: the rest of the Bible makes it clear that *to know God is to meet the Trinity* and *to know God is to be united to Christ*.

KEY TRUTH 1: TO KNOW GOD IS TO MEET THE TRINITY

I pointed out earlier that one of the amazing things about John 17 is that we get to listen in on God's private "family conversation". This is God (the Son) talking to God (the Father). And even that simple statement tells us so much. For a start, it makes it clear that the Father and the Son aren't the same "person". They aren't just God playing different roles. The Father doesn't just morph into the Son when the situation demands. The fact that they are speaking to one another shows that they are clearly distinct. A little earlier in the evening, Jesus spoke to his disciples about the Spirit in a way that shows that he too is a distinct person (for example, in John 14 v 16-17: "And *I* will ask the Father, and *he* will give you another advocate to help you and be with you for ever—the *Spirit* of truth.")

The God of the Bible, it turns out, is like a loving family of three—Father, Son and Holy Spirit—where each member is completely God and completely in step, and yet completely distinct. That's what Christians mean when they talk about God as the Trinity.

For many of us, the idea of the Trinity sounds... well, it sounds weird. God we get. Jesus we get. We may even get the Holy Spirit. But as soon as we start talking about how they "fit together" and using the "T" word (which, as some people are quick to point out, isn't actually used in the Bible), most of us switch off. We'll leave that stuff to the theology nerds, thank you very much. The problem is that if we do that, then not only will our Christian life be severely impoverished, but we will almost certainly lose the plot completely somewhere down the track.

It may seem strange now, but for the first 400 years or so of the Christian church, more energy was poured into working out the right beliefs about (or "doctrine" of) the Trinity than anything else. Men like Irenaeus, Augustine and Athanasius (who were so influential that, like Beyoncé, they only needed one name!) carefully explained what the Father, the Son and the Spirit are like, and how they relate to each other. They did it because they knew that knowing God is at the heart of the Christian life, and so knowing what God is like and how he works really is very important. They made it very clear that *to know God is to meet the Trinity.*

And that's really clear in the rest of Jesus' prayer in John 17. He says to his Father: "I have revealed you to those whom you gave me out of the world [the disciples]. They were yours; you gave them to me and they have obeyed your word" (v 6). Jesus insists that everything that he has achieved is actually down to the Father. Even his message came from his Father: "Now they know that everything you have given me comes from you. For I gave them the words you gave me and they accepted them. They knew with certainty that I came from you, and they believed that you sent me" (v 7-8). In fact, Jesus goes as far as saying that he has nothing apart from his Father: "All I have is yours, and all you have is mine" (v 10). The Father and Son are perfectly in step with each other, and with the Spirit too. When it comes to rescuing us, it is very definitely a team effort.

But it gets even better—because by rescuing us (or, as verse 2 puts it, giving us eternal life), we get to share in this perfect loving, giving relationship! We get to know this God. Here's how Jesus puts it in verse 26: "I have made you known to them [all his followers], and will continue to make you known in order that the love you have for me may be in them and that I myself may be in them". We don't just get to "feel the love"; we are caught up in it! It's not as if we're standing on the edges of the schoolyard, watching a game which looks fun from the outside. We're invited in to play! Not only are we loved by God, but we start to love like God—and this can only happen because the Father, Son and Spirit work so beautifully together.

How does this work? It's not complicated—Jesus introduces us to his Father ("I have made you known to them", v 26). But there is a bit more we can say. Did you notice the little phrase at the end of verse 26? "That I myself may be in them." That's the key. In order to share his knowledge of the Father with us, Jesus Christ the Son "moves in" to our lives through the Spirit, as the Spirit comes to dwell in our hearts. He does it so that we are brought to the heart of God's family. And the great thing about knowing God is that this relationship goes on for ever. (I guess that's why Jesus calls it eternal life.)

So knowing God is not a warm and fuzzy feeling when we close our eyes or sing particular songs; it is a soaring reality which encompasses every part of our minds and hearts. To know God is to be drawn into the warmth and light of the relationships within the Trinity itself—so that we know and share in and delight in God's love. This is what the gospel enables. To know God is no small thing!

And this is something very intimate. If I asked you whether you know the person sitting beside you, what would you say? It could range from "No—I haven't even made eye contact with them yet" to "Yes, they are my best friend, and I would trust them with my life—they know everything about me". When Jesus speaks about us knowing God, he has something more like the latter in mind.

When Christians talk about having a relationship with God, we're not talking about having someone's personal email address or a vague friend-of-a-friend connection. We're not talking about having read about someone or studied them, collecting information about them. When Jesus prays that we might know God, he is shooting for something so far beyond that—he is praying that the Father might draw us to share in the love that he has shared with the Son through the Spirit since before the foundation of the world. We are brought to a place where we could not be more "in". This is huge.

When you're trying to explain to someone what it means when you say you're a Christian, remember this: Christianity is not a mindset or a worldview or a philosophy of life (although it does produce all these). Christianity is founded on and flows from and leads to knowing and enjoying God the Trinity for ever.

KEY TRUTH 2: TO KNOW GOD IS TO BE UNITED WITH CHRIST

All that sounds great. But it should leave us with a question: how can ordinary people like us have a relationship with this totally self-sufficient God? Surely it would be a bit like a human going out for a drink with an ant. God is perfectly happy without us, doesn't need us, and is so far superior to us that we can't even begin to articulate the extent of the gap. How can people like us meet a God like this?

Like many guys, it is a great mystery to me how I managed to marry a woman who is smarter, prettier, wiser and generally nicer than me. The fact that she not only agreed to marry me in the first place but has stuck with me for the past 26 years can only be described as an act of mercy and sacrifice (and if you heard me snore, you'd definitely agree). But for better or worse, she's joined to me: now her family is my family, her stuff is my stuff, and we go through life together.

God forms a relationship with us which is more intimate, more permanent and more satisfying that even the best marriage. And how does this happen? As we saw in John 17 v 26, it happens when Christ "moves in" to bring us life—or, to use the New Testament's favourite way of talking about this, when we are "united to Christ" by faith. From our side, this happens when we hear the gospel, believe it and entrust ourselves to God through Christ. When we do that, something changes for ever—we are joined to Christ permanently.

A little while before Jesus prayed the prayer we've been looking at, he spoke about this reality to his disciples. He compared being united with himself like this to a branch being grafted onto a vine: "I am the vine; you are the branches. If you remain in me and I in you, you will bear much fruit; apart from me you can do nothing" (John 15 v 5). Everything depends on being united to Christ. It is because we are "in Christ" that we can know God and enjoy everything that God has done for us in him. We come to know God through union with Christ.

You may not have thought of it like this before, but it is only because we are "in Christ" that we get all the good stuff that God longs to give us. We can't even approach God on our own, but when we come before God, not merely with Christ but in Christ, we are suddenly able to call the Father "our Father"—we become God's children because we're joined to God's Son, and we share in this relationship of sonship. This is who you are. By grace through faith, we have been inextricably, unbreakably, inseparably joined to the risen Lord Jesus Christ. Nothing can ever separate us from him, reduce us to the status of second-class citizens, or relegate us to the cheap seats—we are his and he is ours.

It's because we are joined to Christ that we get to start enjoying eternal life now. It's because we are united to Christ that his death counts for us. It's because we are joined to Christ that we can be sure that we'll share in a resurrection like his, with a new supernatural body someday. It's because we are "in Christ" that we will—incredibly—get to rule with him over the entire universe for ever in eternity. I'm not sure if you've picked this up, but God's kindness in uniting us to Christ is a very big deal!

So let me spell this out: if you have faith—if you're trusting in the Lord Jesus as King of your life—then YOU ARE united to Christ. And that means that you enjoy all the advantages of the Son's relationship with the Father. Because you are united to Christ, what's true of him is true of you. Together, we share in Christ the Son's relationship with the Father and the Spirit. I don't know about you, but I think that's great!

THE DIFFERENCE THIS MAKES

Here's what we've seen: to know God is to encounter the Trinity through union with Christ. Jesus sums all that up in a very simple phrase (the one we started with): "This is eternal life: that they know [God]" (John 17 v 3). Back in John 10 v 10, Jesus said, "I have come that they may have life, and have it to the full". Now he explains what exactly that life is all about: it is knowing God through being joined to the Son by the Spirit. This is the heart of the Christian life now and will be for ever.

Which leads us to the most important question—so what? What difference does any of this make? We'll spend the rest of this book exploring how these truths are the engine of the gospel-shaped life. But for now, let's look at the difference it makes both to what we should expect, and to what we share.

WHAT WE CAN EXPECT

If God has marshalled all of his resources to make it possible for us to know him through the Lord Jesus Christ, then shouldn't this relationship be the central reality of our lives? Surely it should. But we do need to be quite clear about what the Bible leads us to expect in this relationship. If we are to take a biblical view of knowing God, I think there are three things we can say with absolute confidence about our relationship with God—three components, if you like, which together make up a healthy relationship with God.

First, knowing God is theological. Theology is the study of the truth about God (just as biology is the study of living things or psychology is the study of the mind). Our relationship with God is made possible by the fact that he has *revealed himself* to us through the "living word", the Lord Jesus (which basically means that Jesus is God speaking to us, John 1 v 1), and the written word, the Bible (which shows us Jesus, John 17 v 8). Our relationship begins with God's words, is defined by God's words and is nurtured by God's words, as we'll see more in the next chapter. Do you want to know God better? Then read his word. And read great books about his word. Study theology. Aim high when it comes to thinking about God and relating to God.

Jesus is a person, not a bunch of facts—but he is a person who is known through the Scriptures. It's possible to read the Bible without knowing Jesus any better or deeper. But it's impossible to know Jesus better and deeper without reading the Bible.

Second, knowing God is personal. That may seem almost too obvious to say, but it is worth underlining. God is not like the Force in the *Star Wars* movies. Our God is a Trinity of love who invites us to know and delight in him. Our relationship with God is never individualistic—his plan is to save a whole family of believers—but it really is personal. We are not swallowed up in the great mass of God's people spread across time and space. As Jesus said to his friends, "Are not five sparrows sold for two pennies? Yet not one of them is forgotten by God. Indeed, the very hairs of your head are all numbered. Don't be afraid; you are worth more than many sparrows" (Luke 12 v 6-7).

One of the remarkable things about the Bible is that it is littered with the names of ordinary people from beginning to end. And it is no accident because knowing God is personal. The God of the universe knows you by name and invites you into an eternal relationship with him.

Third, knowing God is experiential. It's something you feel. Now, we need to tread carefully here: we should not be driven by our feelings. That would be fatal. Nor is everyone's temperament or personality the same. I am relatively extroverted—a room full of people gives me a buzz. My friend Katie is more introverted—she'd rather spend her Friday evening having dinner with her flatmate. I react to the world in extremes—most things are either fantastic or awful. My colleague Andrew is more balanced—most things for him are just ok. You get the picture.

Our temperament and personality are generally reflected in our relationship with God. (So if you don't cry much at all, then it's unlikely that every time you pray for people who aren't Christians you'll shed tears. But some people might!) God made us and deals with us as we are. But we cannot escape the fact that knowing God— having a relationship with the Trinity—is experiential. As God speaks to us through his word by his Spirit, it will have some effect on us. In general, it will make us *feel something*: amazed, grateful, happy, sorrowful, humbled, and a hundred other emotions beside. However messed up our emotions and feelings have been by the effects of sin, however tired we are on a given day, whatever we are going through—engaging with God as he reveals himself to us through his word is a real-life event.

Knowing God is theological and personal and experiential. I would go as far as to say that if any of these qualities are missing, then our relationship with God is seriously deficient. We have been made and rescued to know God in this full sense. Do you?

It is, of course, very possible that this is completely foreign to you. Yes, you've been along to church a few times—or perhaps regularly for years. You've read the Bible and maybe a couple of Christian books that one of your mates gave you, but you never realised that the gospel makes it possible to know God in this richest of ways. If that's you, the great news is that God is holding out to you the immeasurable privilege of knowing and enjoying him for ever—do not miss out on that!

Of course, you may have known about all this for years—it's just that you have been slow to take advantage of what God offers. You know it's possible, but you just haven't invested in it at all. Is your "God knowledge" still at an infant's level? Then now would be a great time to step up.

Or perhaps you simply need to hear and take hold of the fact that our God—Father, Son and Spirit—is deeply and personally committed to *you*. God is not a block of wood, and neither are you. So it is perfectly reasonable for us to expect to know God in a way which is theological and personal and experiential.

WHAT WE SHARE

If we've grasped how great these truths are, then inevitably we're going to want to talk about them—especially with those who don't know Jesus. That's a great thing to do! When we do, we need to make sure that the gospel we proclaim is big and high and wide and broad enough. It's not that you've just "got into" church the way that some people might get into cycling. When you chat to your friends about Jesus, what you hold out to people is the offer of knowing the God of the cosmos, the ultimate being, one God in three Persons, who is love in his very nature. It is *this* God who offers us forgiveness, peace, security, satisfaction, freedom and all the other benefits that flow to us through the gospel.

If I had to define the gospel in a tweet, I'd say it is this: *the announcement of what the triune God has done in Christ to make it possible for us to know him and enjoy him for ever.* That is a BIG announcement. Let's make sure that the way we talk about Christianity is positive enough and points to where the Bible points—to the glorious reality of knowing God and delighting in him for ever. You'll probably find that it's sometimes the Christians who've been going the longest that have the smallest view of this message. Don't let that be you.

Knowing God is the ultimate privilege of the gospel, as God joins us to the Lord Jesus and draws us into the very life of the Trinity to share in his love for ever. This is eternal life. And this is what we have every confidence to expect.

2. LIVING WITH GOD IN THE POWER OF THE GOSPEL

"Remember Jesus Christ, raised from the dead,
descended from David. This is my gospel..."
(2 Timothy 2 v 8)

Living as a Christian is actually really simple. It is hard—but it's not complicated.

In fact, it's a bit like playing golf. (I realise that sentence has probably put at least three-quarters of you to sleep, but please stick with me!) Golf is the most difficult game I have ever played. One day it seems so easy, and the next it feels completely impossible.

The annoying thing is that, at its heart, golf is actually very, very simple—all you have to do is swing the club *making sure that when the club makes contact with the ball, it is straight*. That's it. The problem is, of course, that there are so many things that can go wrong: you are standing incorrectly, you are swinging the club too fast/too slowly, your hands are ahead of/behind the ball, you take your eye off the ball, you are off balance, your grip is too loose/too firm... and more!

In other words, golf isn't complicated; it's just hard. And in that, it's exactly like the Christian life.

On one level, living as a Christian is pretty simple. It starts with believing that the gospel—the "good news"—about Jesus is true. As we saw in the last chapter, that good news is "the announcement of what the triune God has done in Christ to make it possible for us to know him and enjoy him for ever".

And then what do we do? Every morning when we get out of bed, we just have to make sure that we have a firm grip on this message—asking for God's help to live in a way which fits with it.

And then what? *Repeat*—every day until God brings us home to live with him in a completely rebooted perfect universe for ever! The gospel is at the heart of becoming a Christian, living as a Christian and keeping going as a Christian.

So the Christian life is simple... but at the same time, it's hard because, as on the golf course, there are so many things that can knock you off course or distract your attention. And when you take your eye off the ball, you end up in the rough.

KEEPING THE MAIN THING THE MAIN THING

So how do we stay focused? One of my favourite statements in the New Testament comes in a letter written by a seasoned preacher, Paul, to his young "apprentice" Timothy, who was a leader of a church in Turkey. As Paul approaches what he suspects will be the end of his life (he was soon to be executed on the order of the Roman Emperor Nero), he tells Timothy to do something unexpectedly simple: "Remember Jesus Christ" (2 Timothy 2 v 8).

At first glance, that actually sounds pretty odd—did Paul think that Timothy might have trouble remembering the name of that teacher guy who had been crucified but refused to stay dead? I think not. Paul is not trying to safeguard Timothy from "early-onset senior moment" syndrome! He is simply reminding his young friend that the Christian life is all about Jesus. We never get past this. We never move on to something else. There is no such thing as advanced Christianity. It's always all about what Jesus has done for us by becoming one of us, dying instead of us and blasting his way through death so that we might live for him.

Paul's statement goes on to underline two things about Jesus: "Remember Jesus Christ, raised from the dead, descended from David". It sounds pretty simple, but Paul has actually managed to cram the entire message of the Bible into ten words!

First, Jesus was "raised from the dead". Jesus' death wasn't the sad and tragic end to his life—it was the purpose and highpoint of his mission to earth. Jesus came to sacrifice himself for us. A perfect man who lived a perfect life chose to face the anger we should have faced and the punishment that we had earned. But did Jesus' sacrifice "work"? Would God accept it? The fact that God raised Jesus from the dead is his big "YES!" to those questions. So Paul encourages Timothy to remember the fact that by beating death and rising again, Jesus has opened the way for us to know God for ever.

Second, Jesus was "descended from David". This is important for two very different reasons. On the one hand, it makes it very obvious that Jesus was a flesh-and-blood kind of guy, just like us—he was a real human with human ancestors. So he really did live, die and rise from death. (He wasn't a ghost or some kind of superhuman.) On the other hand, he was God's chosen King. Back in around 1000 BC, God had told King David of Israel that one of his descendants would be the ultimate King, who would set up a kingdom that would last for ever. (You can read about that in 2 Samuel 7.) The New Testament makes it very clear that Jesus was that King, and his death and resurrection led to his enthronement as the King of the universe, alongside his Father. Although it may not always look like it now, Jesus Christ does rule the universe, and one day that will become very obvious as he returns to straighten everything out.

At this point, you might be thinking, "But didn't we already cover this stuff about Jesus in chapter 1?" Well spotted!

Yes, we did, but it's so important that it's worth saying it again. Knowing God and enjoying him for ever is the goal of the gospel, but the gospel itself is the announcement of all that God has done for us in Christ. It is his death and resurrection which make it possible for us to enter a relationship with God in Christ.

So to sum it up: if we want to live a "gospel-shaped life" then, we need to remember Jesus Christ—that is, to remember the gospel. But how do we do that?

WHAT HAPPENS WHEN YOU FORGET YOU'RE A DAD

I have to confess that sometimes over the years I have forgotten that I am a dad. I don't mean that one of my three daughters shows up at the breakfast table and I wonder why there is a stranger in our house, or that I forget their names (although, allegedly, I have, on occasion, got them mixed up... with the name of the dog!). I mean that I have forgotten that I am a dad *and that this should shape everything that I do.*

This "forgetting" may have meant taking my phone to the park and answering emails when I was supposed to be lifting a little girl on and off the climbing frame. Or responding to a plea for help with algebra by saying, "I'll be with you in a minute", and then getting so engrossed in what I was doing that I forgot all about it. Or, worst of all, realising that I was still at work, despite saying that I would pick the girls up from their music lesson!

That's the kind of forgetting that Paul is concerned about. It's easy to forget from moment to moment that we are people who have been brought to new life in Christ and will enjoy him for ever. When we lose it with someone, or we drift through the day without thinking about who Christ is, or we opt for some "(all about) me time", we forget Jesus.

So we need to remember Jesus Christ because if we don't remember him, we'll forget him! Which is where the Bible comes in.

MEET THE TALKING GOD

From the beginning of the Bible, it's clear that God is a *talking God*. He creates the world and the first humans (in Genesis 1), and the next thing God does is to speak to them (Genesis 2 – 3). As the world goes rapidly downhill under the effects of sin, God confides in another person, Noah, whom he rescues (by telling him to build a large boat/ark) before hitting "reset" on the world with a flood (Genesis 6 – 9). A few generations later, God speaks directly to someone living in ancient Mesopotamia called Abram and tells him to move country because he and his wife Sarai are a key part of God's plans to make an entire people who know and love him (Genesis 12). I could go on (and on, and on!) but you get the picture. This God talks.

The Old Testament is basically the story of God talking to his special people, Israel—and of his people pretty much ignoring what he says. As history continues, God speaks directly to people like Moses (to whom he gave the Ten Commandments); and King David (whom we mentioned earlier); and to a long procession of prophets (spokesmen sent by God to tell people what he is like and how to relate to him). No one could possibly fault God for his efforts to speak to his people—the problem is that they won't (or can't) listen and do what he says! Which is why God speaks a different kind of word...

In one of the most dramatic starts to a book ever, the apostle John, one of Jesus' closest friends, introduces us to that different kind of word:

> [1] In the beginning was the Word, and the Word was with God, and the Word was God. [2] He was with God in the beginning. [3] Through him all things were made; without him nothing was made that has been made. (John 1 v 1-3)

It's not just that the Word has been around for ever. John goes on to explain that this Word is now a living, breathing person on the planet. This Word is Jesus Christ himself: "The Word became flesh and made his dwelling among us. We have seen his glory, the glory of the one and only Son, who came from the Father, full of grace and truth" (John 1 v 14).

So if the Word is Jesus, then why the weird code name? Well, think about what words do. If I want to get to know someone, I need to listen to them talk—it's as they speak that I discover who they are, where they've come from, what they're like and the things they're passionate about. Standing together in a room in silence won't do much good. I need to hear their words.

That's why Jesus is the Word. He's the culmination of everything that God has said in the Old Testament. He shows us who God is, what he's like and the things he cares about. Later in the New Testament, the writer to the Hebrews explains it like this: "In the past God spoke to our ancestors through the prophets at many times and in various ways, but in these last days he has spoken to us by his Son" (Hebrews 1 v 1-2).

So how do we hear the talking God today? The simple answer is in Jesus.

And how do we encounter Jesus? There's a simple answer to that too: through the Bible.

ONE BOOK, ONE SUBJECT
The Bible is all about Jesus. The Old Testament (the bit written before Jesus was on earth) promised what God *would do* through Jesus. And the New Testament (the bit written after Jesus was on earth) proclaims what God *has done* through Jesus. So every time we open the Bible, we're reading about Jesus; we're being reminded of the gospel.

Jesus himself made that claim. Luke 24 records a slightly embarrassing incident that happened after Jesus' resurrection, involving two of his friends: Cleopas and another disciple whose name we're not told (I suspect that it was Cleopas' wife, and that he lovingly asked Luke to leave out her name to spare her—but I could be wrong!). This pair spent an afternoon and evening with the risen Jesus without recognising who they were talking to. When it finally dawned on them, they had the huge thrill of listening to Jesus himself explain what had just happened in his death and resurrection:

[25] [Jesus] said to them, "How foolish you are, and how slow to believe all that the prophets have spoken! [26] Did not the Messiah have to suffer these things and then enter his glory?" [27] And beginning with Moses and all the Prophets, he explained to them what was said in all the Scriptures concerning himself.

(Luke 24 v 25-27)

Basically, Jesus explained that he was the one the Old Testament had been talking about, pointing to and waiting for!

That's exactly what Paul says in a classic passage from the same letter to Timothy that we looked at earlier in this chapter:

[14] But as for you, continue in what you have learned and have become convinced of, because you know those from whom you learned it, [15] and how from infancy you have known the Holy Scriptures, which are able to make you wise for salvation through faith in Christ Jesus. [16] All Scripture is God-breathed and is useful for teaching, rebuking, correcting and training

in righteousness, [17] so that the servant of God may be thoroughly equipped for every good work.

(2 Timothy 3 v 14-17)

Paul says that the way we find out how to become Christians is by reading the Bible (v 14). But he doesn't stop there: reading the Bible is also the key to keeping going as Christians (v 15). And he isn't finished yet: God uses the Bible to grow us in our understanding and maturity as Christians (v 16). And there's one more: it's the Bible which gives us the words to say to other people (v 17). That's why reading and getting to grips with the Bible is such a big deal.

At one level, reading the Bible works like reading any other book. For a start, we need to be able to understand the language it's written in—which is why it's been translated from its original languages (mainly Hebrew and Greek) into English. Then we need to be able to work out the meaning of a sentence, spot the main point of a paragraph, and put a statement in its context (which is what you do with any other piece of writing, mostly without really thinking about it).

But in another sense, the Bible is unlike any other book: it is "God-breathed" (v 16). The Bible has both human authors, like Paul, and a divine author—God himself. God "inspired" these guys as they wrote so that even though they still sound like themselves, their words also come with God's wisdom, power and authority. It was the Holy Spirit who helped them write, and it's the Holy Spirit who helps us to understand and read today. It's not that God spoke a few thousand years ago and now we've got the transcript—or that we're watching some hollow home video from a bygone era. Instead, in a very real way, God continues to speak now, through the Spirit, as we read his word: "The word of God is alive and active" (Hebrews 4 v 12). That's why Paul told one group of Christians that when he preached, he did so "not in words taught us by human wisdom but in words taught by the Spirit, explaining spiritual realities with Spirit-taught words" (1 Corinthians 2 v 13). The words were clearly Paul's at one level but were used by the Spirit to introduce people to the truth about Jesus.

The Bible, then, is the tool which the Spirit uses to show us and remind us of the "gospel"—what God the Father and Jesus Christ the Son have done, are doing and will do for us.

This is a truth that makes sense of some of the things you'll have experienced already in your venture into the weird world of being a Christian. For example, this is why someone probably prays before the sermon at church on a Sunday, asking for God's help. And it's why some of your friends and family, no matter how many times you tell them or bring them to church, just don't see what you see in the Bible—because reading the Bible is not an intellectual thing but a spiritual thing. It's not magic, but it is spiritual—and wonderfully, God can and does work through the Bible to bring people to new life and maturity in Christ.

THE BIBLE AND THE GOSPEL-SHAPED LIFE

Telling Christians that they need to read the Bible is hardly a new idea. But I reckon that often, even when we are told to read the Bible, we have no real idea why, other than a vague sense that it will be "good for us". But so is eating vegetables! Yet our attitude to reading the Bible will be totally different when we grasp that the Bible is how God speaks to us, helping us to remember Jesus Christ.

Knowing this will (or should!) drive us out of bed in the morning, eager to get all the help we need for the day ahead by being reminded of the gospel as we read the Bible. When we fall into bed at the end of the day, we'll go back to God for the resources we need (the forgiveness, peace, joy) to deal with everything that has happened to us during the day, and to process all the wise and the stupid things we have done. We'll do our best never to miss church because we know that's the place where we hear what God has to say to us as a church family. We'll do anything to avoid missing our home group (or whatever we call the bunch of people we meet up with between Sundays to read the Bible and pray together) because we know we need the gospel. And I should tell you upfront: *we never, ever get past this.*

Many years ago, someone from the church where I was pastor told me that she hated my preaching, largely because all my talks were the same. I have to say I'm not always at my best in these situations, and I tend to get defensive. But for once, I managed to resist that temptation and simply said, "Thank you very much". This seemed to throw her! When she asked me to explain, I said that I was sorry if I had bored her but that I happily admitted to being a "one trick pony". Every Bible teacher should be because, although the gospel is rich and multi-faceted, and so beautiful we can never either exhaust it or do it justice, it is, at heart, a relatively simple announcement. It's what *the triune God has done in Christ to make it possible for us to know him and enjoy him for ever*. And in a very real sense, that's all we've got. We never get past it, or fully grasp it, or move on from it.

Our loving God invites us into new life through the gospel. He patiently and gently trains us to live for him through the gospel. He gives us the power to live the Christian life through the gospel. He enables us to keep going as a Christian through the gospel. That's why reading the Bible matters—because the gospel matters, and it's through the Bible that God speaks the gospel into our lives.

YOU ARE NOT ALONE! PRAYER AND THE GOSPEL-SHAPED LIFE

And one more thing... God doesn't just do all this for the sake of it. It's because he wants to draw us into relationship with him: God speaks to us; we speak to him. This is what prayer is: speaking to God our Father. Real prayer isn't a form of meditation that twists God's arm; nor is it just good for our mental health! It's about enjoying our relationship with our loving heavenly Father. You don't need special words or a specific agenda—you're free to talk to him about whatever's on your mind.

One of the things we'll want to do when we speak to God is ask for his help. John Calvin—a pastor in the 16th century—once wrote, "Just as faith is born through the gospel, through the gospel our hearts are trained to call on God's name." In other words, when we are confronted by what God has done for us in Christ, the most natural thing in the world is to ask for his help to live out these gospel realities.

I once wrote a book which examined every prayer in the Bible—surprisingly, they all do basically the same thing: they ask God to do what he has already promised in the gospel (now you really don't need to read the book!). This is essentially what Jesus says about prayer in Matthew 7:

> [7] Ask and it will be given to you; seek and you will find; knock and the door will be opened to you. [8] For everyone who asks receives; the one who seeks finds; and to the one who knocks, the door will be opened.
>
> [9] Which of you, if your son asks for bread, will give him a stone? [10] Or if he asks for a fish, will give him a snake? [11] If you, then, though you are evil, know how to give good gifts to your children, how much more will your Father in heaven give good gifts to those who ask him! (Matthew 7 v 7-11)

Our God is poised to give us what we ask for... when we ask for what he has promised. So what has he promised?

The Bible says that God will do all kinds of things that we can't do for ourselves. God has promised to rescue us from the things that could harm us eternally; to give us strength to live for him; to use every circumstance to grow us to be more like Christ; to give us words to say when we are being made to suffer because we're following Jesus; to forgive us when we have sinned. And wonderfully, when we ask God to do any of this gospel-shaped stuff, he does it—because it's what he's promised to do.

Reading the Bible is important because God speaks the gospel into our lives through it. Praying is important because, once we see what God is asking of us, we'll realise we need God's help to pull it off. And the great news is that he's poised to help.

BUT WHAT DO I DO NOW?

I'm guessing that most people reading this book are either relatively new to this "being a Christian" thing, or are suddenly starting to take it more seriously. And if that's the case, you can be forgiven for thinking that the Bible is long (it is!), difficult (not as difficult as you might think) and scary (only a little bit). So where on earth do we start?

Reading the Bible regularly for yourself is pretty important. There are lots of fantastic resources out there to help you get started (see page 117 for some suggestions). But it's also good to remember that reading the Bible with other people is vital too (in fact, most of the New Testament was written for small-ish groups of people to read together).

And make sure that your week is kicked off every Sunday by hearing the Bible explained by someone who has poured their energies into understanding and living it themselves, and passing it on to other people as they preach. I'm sure that person would also be delighted to suggest lots of other resources or groups that can help you get into the Bible too.

When it comes down to it, the Christian life might be hard, but it isn't all that complicated. God himself speaks to us by the Spirit through his word, working the gospel of the Lord Jesus deeper into our hearts and minds. And what do we do? We ask for God to do what he has promised as we pray. And then we repeat! This is the gospel-shaped life.

There is plenty more to say about how this works out. (In fact it will happily occupy us for the rest of our lives!) But it's important to realise that we never get past this. It's how we start the Christian life and how we'll make it to the end—and it's what we need for all the days in between. No wonder Paul says, "Remember Jesus Christ".

3. KNOWING
OURSELVES THROUGH
THE GOSPEL

"Humble yourselves before the Lord, and he will lift you up." (James 4 v 10)

I grew up in Northern Ireland, but I now live in Australia. When I arrived here, I was warned that the Brisbane traffic police are notoriously strict. So every day for three years I drove to work along the same route, making very sure to stay at 60 kph (40 mph). In fact, I have to say I was a little smug about my careful observation of the rules of the road. Then I got an ominously official letter in the mail. And the next day, I got another. And three days later, I got another. Each of them informed me that in a single inglorious week, I had been recorded driving at 60 *in a 50 kph (30 mph) zone.*

I can barely describe the sinking feeling in my stomach. The money. The penalty points. The shame. The prospect of my licence being suspended. Even writing about it brings me out in a cold sweat all over again! I had thought I was a law-abiding citizen. But in that moment, I was exposed.

Most of us have these kind of "Oh no!" moments from time to time. You can probably think of a time when you suddenly realised you had been caught out or exposed. Sometimes they're more serious than a speeding ticket; mainly we do our best to avoid them. Yet the uncomfortable truth that's at the heart of this chapter is that while the gospel is good news, it also has the effect of making us feel very exposed.

So far, we've seen how great it is that, through the death and resurrection of the Lord Jesus Christ, it's possible for ordinary, messed-up people like you and me to know God. Now we get to live a gospel-shaped life with him as he speaks to us through his word and as we speak to him in prayer. That's a very big deal!

The problem is that once we have grasped that, sooner or later a very troubling thought will start to nag away at us: God may be good, pure and kind (or, to use the Bible's preferred words, *holy* and *glorious*)... but what about us? Compared to him we start to feel a bit uncomfortable. Exposed.

The 16th-century theologian John Calvin wrote a book to sum up the Bible's teaching about life, the universe and everything, called the *Institutes of the Christian Religion*.

Right at the start of the book, we find this sentence: "Nearly all wisdom we possess, that is to say, true and sound wisdom, consists of two parts: the knowledge of God and of ourselves" (Inst. I.1.i). Calvin's basic insight is that knowing God leads inevitably to discovering the truth about ourselves—and that is never pretty. Just to make sure we've got this, Calvin goes on to point out that meeting God in Christ reveals our "shaming nakedness", which exposes "a teeming horde of infirmities". (We normally just call all this "sin".) That's why, he adds, we will only begin to seek after God when "we begin to become displeased with ourselves".

Living a gospel-shaped life with the God of the Bible is both hugely ennobling *and* deeply confronting. The great news is that because we are secure "in Christ", facing the truth about ourselves becomes much less threatening. So as people who know God in Christ through the gospel, let's take a look at ourselves with the help of James 4 v 1-10.

LIFE IN THE MESS

The book of James is a letter written by Jesus' half-brother, James; after Jesus died, rose and ascended back to heaven, James went on to become a leader of the church in Jerusalem. He wrote the letter to help God's people scattered across the Mediterranean area to live a gospel-shaped life.

Chapter 4 deals with the moment-by-moment reality of life as the people of God. And it isn't pretty:

¹ What causes fights and quarrels among you? Don't they come from your desires that battle within you? ² You desire but do not have, so you kill. You covet but you cannot get what you want, so you quarrel and fight. You do not have because you do not ask God. ³ When you ask, you do not receive, because you ask with wrong motives, that you may spend what you get on your pleasures.

⁴ You adulterous people, don't you know that friendship with the world means enmity against God? Therefore, anyone who chooses to be a friend of the world becomes an enemy of God. (James 4 v 1-4)

I don't think there is any passage in the New Testament which gets us to the heart of the matter quite so quickly, or so bluntly, as this one.

James says to these Christians, *How come there are problems in your church? It's because of you!* More specifically, he says it's because of *what they want*—because of their "desires" (v 1)—that they run into trouble. Relationships in this church are so bad that James says they are metaphorically killing each other (v 2). James' point is that we are hard-wired to be selfish, and that isn't good.

These Christians have been forgiven, but they are still sinful. And I expect you've seen that in yourself and Christians you know too. We may have been joined to Christ, but we are still flawed, sinful human beings. And how does that show? It shows in all kinds of disordered desires. We want all the wrong things, and we don't want the right things. And more than that, we choose the wrong things. There are times when we want to be selfish or mean; when we long for more stuff than we have; when we just want to be right. And all too often, because we want the wrong things, we choose the wrong things. The problem is deep in us, and the gospel shows that up very clearly.

All this may come as a bit of a shock. Many of us grew up in an environment where we were encouraged to think that we are fundamentally good people, with no limits to what we can achieve. In Australia, most schools have mottos. Our girls have attended schools with mottos such as "Act well your part", "Yours the future" and "Knowledge is power". The message is clear: *you can do anything you like*. The problem is that this isn't true. It's like the gold-medal-winning Olympic athlete declaring in their breathless post-event interview that it just goes to show what's possible if you believe in yourself, train hard and never give up. That's fine if you're young, athletic and over 6 feet tall—but I am none of those things! So, however hard I try, a win at the Olympics is beyond me (as is, for that matter, a Nobel science prize). Our culture's relentlessly positive thinking just doesn't fit with reality; we are a messed-up part of a very messed-up world.

The Bible says that our Christian lives will be marked by two things that it calls *sin* and *temptation*. The marvellous thing, however, is that God gives us the "tools" we need to deal with this danger—*repentance* and *faith*. If we are to live a gospel-shaped life in our broken world, we need to make sure that we get what both pairs of realities are all about.

SIN AND TEMPTATION

As we've already seen, James spells out what life is like for us pretty clearly: "What causes fights and quarrels among you? Don't they come from your desires that battle within you?" (4 v 1) What happens when you put two people who are driven by their misdirected desires in the same room? Simple. If I'm living for me, and you are living for you, then it is all going to end in tears (v 2). But that isn't the end of James' diagnosis.

Beneath our self-centred desires, there is a basic mistake in our thinking: we think that the way to be happy is to get what we want. But God says that the way to be happy is to take what he gives—to understand that God has promised us everything we need in the Lord Jesus and will follow through on that promise. Instead we ignore or reject what God has done because we are too proud or too stubborn to trust him. And even when we do ask God for stuff, it's all about us, not him: "When you ask, you do not receive, because you ask with wrong motives, that you may spend what you get on your pleasures" (4 v 3). We make it all about us—which is why James describes his readers as "adulterous people". When we say, "I choose me", we are rejecting God.

And this is what makes sin so serious. Perhaps by now you're thinking, "Ok, I can be a little selfish sometimes. But why is that such a big deal?" It's because for God, this is all intensely personal. That's why James uses the language of adultery. It's like one spouse saying to the other, "I'm having an affair, but it's not that serious. I'm still around for you at the weekends." No—any betrayal is a personal rejection. And while God is a faithful husband who, as we'll see, remains committed to his adulterous people, our sinful patterns damage the quality of that relationship.

Right from the beginning of the Bible, sin has always been about rejecting the King who made us. In its opening chapters, Genesis 1 – 3, things go catastrophically wrong for the newly created human race when the first couple, Adam and Eve, decide to do what seems best to them rather than what God has told them. In choosing their way, not God's, they do exactly what James is talking about—they make themselves God's enemies, betraying his love and trust in a form of "spiritual adultery".

I really hope you get the implications of this. The gospel-shaped life is one which takes seriously the horrible truth about what we are actually like. There is nothing naïve or defensive or self-protective or arrogant or hypocritical about authentic Christianity because the gospel reveals what we are truly like: we are so precious to God that he sent Christ to die for us, but we are so rebellious that he *had* to die for us.

As human beings, we are driven by all kinds of passions and desires, which all boil down to the same basic thing. As we try to live for Jesus, there will be plenty of external temptations, but the main game is internal: it's battling these desires which scream in our inner ear, "Do it, do it, do it for YOU".

Do you realise that this is what you are up against, all day, every day? Have you understood that even if you have belonged to Christ for years, inside you is still a knot of selfish desires? Do you realise that if provoked in the right way, at the right time, you will become a living example of what James is talking about? Do you sense that you are never more than an instant away from making stupid and sinful choices for the simple reason that you still like sinning? This is life in the mess. We need to get that saying "no" to ourselves and "yes" to Christ—dealing with sin and temptation—is the main game when it comes to Christianity.

THE TEMPTATIONS I BATTLE

Before I wrote this section, I took some time to try to identify and face up to the strong desires that I live with. It wasn't a pleasant experience! This is what I came up with:

I have a very strong desire to prove myself. Growing up, I desperately wanted to make my parents proud of me. At school and college, I wanted to do well. Now I really want to be able to say to myself, "Yes, you are a good husband and dad". I would also really like to do a decent job on this book. Deep down, I think that if I manage this, then I will be able to pat myself on the back and go to sleep happy.

I have a very strong desire to be right. I wish it were different, but it isn't. (Ask my family, my friends and my colleagues.) I have a very deep-rooted habit of asserting my opinion with a force which bears no relation to the factual basis of what I'm saying! The reality that I am often wrong has, sadly, done little to dent my confidence over the years.

I have a very strong desire to be accepted and liked. For someone so pig-headed (see the previous paragraph), I have a surprisingly strong desire to be liked and accepted. It matters too much to me whether you like this book. It matters too much to me what my workmates and the guys on my football team and everyone I know thinks of me. It's a very real pull for me, and it makes it hard to have difficult conversations and to make tough calls.

I have a very strong desire to be first. "Morning tea" is a great Australian tradition—basically, it's when we eat food in the middle of the morning. Occasionally, I find myself thinking that if I left my office a few minutes early or stopped teaching a little early, I would beat the crowd and get to the chocolate biscuits before the students. In addition, board games bring out the worst in me. Enough said.

I have a very strong desire to indulge myself. I work pretty hard. My danger has always been to work too hard rather than not hard enough. But when I have worked really hard, I find myself having to cope with a very serious case of "but I deserve X" syndrome. I deserve to collapse on the couch, or eat a large bag of chips, or switch off relationally... So that's what I do, regardless of what anyone else needs from me.

I have a very strong desire to be appreciated. I don't like a lot of fuss, and I certainly don't like to be made a fuss of. Until, that is, people don't make a fuss of me. Then I feel it acutely. What's wrong with me?! I *really* want to be praised and thanked and celebrated... *on my terms*.

These are (just some of) my strong desires. And that's just one person on one day! You'll be different. Not better or worse but different.

So why does all this matter? It matters because coming to terms with our selfish desires will stop us explaining away our actions, and it will stop us justifying ourselves all the time. We'll admit that our default is to get it badly, sinfully wrong. In fact, we'll realise that we are completely incapable of pulling off a completely pure act. Even if we ever managed to do a truly good and pure thing entirely for the glory of God, we would inevitably blow it by patting ourselves on the back for being so humble and selfless!

So have you got your head around Side A of life in the mess? The gospel exposes our sin and the reality of temptation. But it also reassures us that we have been united to Christ by faith. In other words, we live as "forgiven sinners". This is who we are—which takes us to Side B.

REPENTANCE AND FAITH

The great news is that God does not leave us to wallow in our deep dysfunction. He sees it, he longs for it to be different, and he acts to change it. James continues:

> [5] Or do you think Scripture says without reason that he jealously longs for the spirit he has caused to dwell in us? [6] But he gives us more grace. (James 4 v 5-6)

The beauty of the gospel is not simply that God forgives us but that he gives us a way out—he transforms us through the painful recognition, exposure and overcoming of our sin. In James' words, "he gives us more grace". Grace is undeserved, gospel-shaped help. It's a quick way of saying that even though we don't deserve anything, God has given us everything we need in Christ. And how do we get this grace? How does it flow to us? The answer that James gives can be summed up in a single word: *repentance*. That is, a 180-degree turn from going our own way to going God's way.

On October 31st 1517 Martin Luther kicked off what he thought would be a theological discussion with his university colleagues by nailing "95 theses"—theological statements—to the church door in Wittenberg, Germany (an event which eventually spiralled into a whole continent-wide movement called the Reformation). Luther's very first "thesis" was a game-changer: "When our Lord and Master Jesus Christ said, 'Repent', he willed the entire life of believers to be one of repentance". When it comes to a gospel-shaped life, repentance is where it begins.

James lays down this same principle, underlining the need for repentance by quoting the Old Testament:

That is why Scripture says: "God opposes the proud but shows favour [or grace] to the humble."

(v 6, quoting Proverbs 3 v 34)

Then James goes on to tell us to do it in seven different ways in 4 v 7-10, piling up pictures that expose our innate weakness:

1. "Submit yourselves, then, to God."

2. "Resist the devil, and he will flee from you."

3. "Come near to God and he will come near to you."

4. "Wash your hands, you sinners, and purify your hearts, you double-minded."

5. "Grieve, mourn and wail."

6. "Change your laughter to mourning and your joy to gloom."

7. "Humble yourselves before the Lord, and he will lift you up."

What's he saying? *Admit that God is the boss and you aren't. Face the fact that you are siding with the evil one. Run to God now. Stop sinning and throw yourselves on God. Take your stupidity seriously. Stop laughing and wise up. Bow before your God and King.* Take your pick. The overall message is clear: *Repent. Own your sin and run back to God.*

I suspect that for many of us, our greatest need is to live lives of repentance. Show me someone who is not repenting, day by day, week by week, and I'll show you someone who is proud and who is not living out the gospel of the Lord Jesus.

So here's the picture: even as Christians, every day we are fighting what is often a losing battle with our desires. We are choosing "me", over and over again. And according to verse 7, the devil, also known as Satan or the evil one, is also persistently encouraging us to do our own thing rather than obey God. The Bible doesn't have a whole lot to say about the evil one, other than mentioning that he hates God, constantly tries to undermine God and his work by getting at us, and that he has been soundly and permanently defeated by Jesus' death and resurrection (Colossians 2 v 15). But that doesn't stop him trying to cause as much havoc as he can.

And what is God doing while all this is going on? He is speaking to us day after day after day: wooing, pursuing, explaining, insisting, demanding a wholehearted response —a response that affects every atom of our being, every corner of our lives, every gram of our resources. He has given us the Spirit, who dwells in us to move us and shape us and change us. So what must we do? We must listen. We must repent. Over and over again.

Because sin is always trying to make a comeback in our lives, the Christian life will *always* be one of repentance. So what does that actually look like? J. I. Packer's book

A Passion for Holiness helpfully explains the "nuts and bolts" of repentance like this:

- Realistic recognition that we have wronged God

- Regretful remorse at having dishonoured God

- Reverent requesting of God's pardon

- Resolute renunciation of sin

- Requisite restitution to those we have hurt

In other words, when real repentance happens, the tears are real, the words are humble, the determination is obvious, and the change—and the relief—is real.

So what do you need to repent of? Really we should always have an answer to this question on the tip of our tongues. If you aren't aware of sin issues in your life right now, it can only be because you aren't thinking or because you are kidding yourself. Repentance needs to be specific and decisive. And it really matters because the wonderful thing is that repentance is the first step to real change.

So what's the second step? The biblical twin of repentance is faith. Look again at what James tells us to do: "Submit yourselves, then, to God ... Come near to God ... Humble yourselves before the Lord." There is more here than simply admitting our sin and turning back to God. James is calling us to exercise *faith*.

So what is "faith"? It's another of those little words which has a lot packed into it! Lots of people today think of faith as something weak and vaguely mystical. But nothing could be further from the truth. Faith is truth-driven, reality-facing, robust trust in the Lord of the universe. Very simply, faith is believing that God will do what he's said he will do. To have faith is to believe that what God has said is true (that Jesus has paid for our sin) and to do what he tells us. Faith, then, is to *believe the gospel*—it is to trust God and *put our full weight on him*.

The beautiful promise is that when we do that, God *will* forgive us—truly and totally. Don't miss the words at the end of James 4 v 10: "Humble yourselves before the Lord, *and he will lift you up*". Sometimes we find that hard to believe. You'll probably get to a point in your Christian life where you mess things up so monumentally that you'll wonder how you can possibly come back from it. When that happens, this is the promise we need to hold on to. *We* might be worse than we ever imagined—"but *he* gives us more grace" (v 6).

The moment-by-moment real-time dynamic of the gospel-shaped life is driven by *repentance*—running back to God—and *faith*—believing the gospel and throwing our weight on Christ, trusting him for the resources we need to live for him. If we are Christians, we live by faith: not in the sense that we reject logic or common sense in favour of wishful thinking, but in that our every step is dominated by what God has done for us in Christ. It is our delight in God in response to the gospel, and the acknowledgment of our own weakness in light of the gospel, which drives us to trust Christ and not ourselves. He is our strength.

THE DIFFERENCE THIS MAKES

Our sin is real and horrible and powerful, but not beyond the reach of Jesus, who holds out forgiveness even as he calls us to repent and trust him. These are the marks of spiritual health.

Embracing who we are comes as such a relief! Getting to know ourselves through the gospel does five things at least:

1. It frees us to be honest before God. He has an intimate, perfect and exhaustive knowledge of what we are like. And once we get that, there's no point in pretending any more. Jesus Christ—the second Person of the Trinity—has already had to face God's wrath on our behalf. There isn't really any dignity left to preserve, so we might as well be honest!

2. It is the key to humility. Because we have faced the truth about ourselves, there is no need for us to look down on others, or talk ourselves up, or try to massage our image. We are who we are.

3. It produces an enduring sense of awe. The longer we go on, the more amazed we are by God's beauty and splendour, by our own capacity to be ratbags, and by Jesus' ability to bridge that gap.

4. It creates real tenderness towards others. When we face how broken we are, we are more sympathetic to the struggles and stupidity of other people. There are fewer surprises, less disappointment, less condescension. In short, we are much easier to be around.

5. It enables us to be of real help to one another. We can speak truth to one another without being judgmental or patronising. It brings us all to the same level and highlights that we all need the same thing—to be reminded of the gospel and to be moved to repentance and faith.

This, then, is the gospel-shaped life: a life of knowing God and being known by God, in all the unnerving comfort that this brings. There will be plenty of "Oh no" moments as we realise the depths of our sin and temptation; but on offer for every one is a "Yes, Jesus" moment, as we come to him in repentance and faith. And there is nothing sweeter than that.

4. BEING TRANSFORMED BY THE GOSPEL

"Therefore we do not lose heart. Though outwardly we are wasting away, yet inwardly we are being renewed day by day." (2 Corinthians 4 v 16)

Fiona and I have been married for 26 years and counting. She is my best friend, the person who has had the biggest influence on my life, the one I love spending time with above all others. But I have to say, our marriage didn't get off to the best start.

We had our first fight on honeymoon. And for me, that was the signal that our marriage was over! My parents had an ultra-calm relationship—I can't remember them ever having anything approaching a row. As a result I expected that my marriage would likewise be a sea of tranquillity. Even though my wife-to-be and I were both strong-minded, vocal people, I still thought that calm would magically descend once we said, "I do". So when we had that argument on honeymoon, I plummeted into the depths of despair. I was already working out how I would break the news to our parents, and thinking through an equitable way to divide up the wedding presents. As far as I was concerned, it was over. I had blown it. Period.

And Fiona? She was actually quite pleased. She had a far more realistic idea of what an adult relationship looks like, and had embraced this hiccup as a normal growth opportunity. Thankfully, she talked me down from my apocalyptic ledge, and we're still together.

Expectations are very, very important. That's true of marriage, and it's also true of the Christian life. When it comes to the nuts-and-bolts, moment-to-moment daily experience of living with and for Jesus, *what exactly do you expect?* That's what we're looking at in this chapter: what the gospel-shaped life *looks like and feels like*.

Most Christians tend to fall into one of two equal and opposite errors. For some of us, the danger is that we *expect far too much* of the Christian life—we think that following Jesus will make life much easier and happier, and that everyone will love us. We'll never get sick (or at least, not *really* sick), we'll always have loads of money, and life will be just lovely. This view is reinforced by the overblown claims of some Bible teachers promising everything from a perfect marriage partner to a bulging investment portfolio and private jet if we will only believe hard enough.

But for many of us, I suspect, the danger is that we *expect far too little* from the Christian life—we just focus on trying to keep our heads above water. At most, we are dreaming of limping along a little faster! Following Jesus isn't much more than gritting our teeth and waiting for heaven. This isn't helped, of course, by the fact that Christianity has taken a bit of a battering in the public sphere in the last few years.

So what can we actually expect in real time? Is perfection within our grasp? Or is any kind of change beyond us? Should we feel happy? Act "happy"? Prepare to be miserable until we die? Our expectations hang on the answers to these questions.

GOD'S AGENDA FOR CHANGE

So far, we've seen how, through the gospel, God introduces us to himself and shows us ourselves, moving us to repentance and faith. But this isn't just an endless cycle. In fact, it's more of an upward spiral: in this chapter we'll see that *God expects us to be transformed by the gospel through the Spirit*. Even better, *he is committed to making this happen*. Our experience of the Christian life should be one of *gradual but real transformation* and *deepening joy*, even though life is often hard. Over time, we can expect God to make a real and obvious difference in our lives.

2 Corinthians is probably Paul's most intensely personal and passionate letter. He's writing to tackle a hugely messy situation in a church he set up years before. As he does that, he gives us a unique insight into the reality of living as servants of the Lord Jesus.

Paul starts by describing in dramatic language what God has done in and for the church family at Corinth. At that time, travelling preachers would bring a letter of recommendation when they visited churches, in order to prove that they were legit. But Paul says that the Corinthians themselves are the only reference he needs. They are "a letter from Christ, the result of our ministry, written not with ink but with the Spirit of the living God, not on tablets of stone but on tablets of human hearts" (2 Corinthians 3 v 3). In other words, the Spirit himself has brought about real change in these believers.

Paul goes on to contrast what happened when God spoke to his people on Mount Sinai in the Old Testament with what has happened now that God has spoken to us through Jesus. In Exodus 19 and 20 Moses went up Mount Sinai to receive the Ten Commandments from God, written on stone tablets. When God spoke, there was fire and smoke and an earthquake. It was all terrifyingly impressive.

But Paul makes the point that while Sinai was great, it didn't change anyone. Even Moses—who had such a stunning experience of God's glory that his face shone when he came down from the mountain—found that the glow wore off over time. Now, though, God changes all his people by the Spirit as the message of the gospel is explained:

And we all ... are being transformed into his image with ever-increasing glory, which comes from the Lord, who is the Spirit. (2 Corinthians 3 v 18)

Our experience is one of being constantly made more and more like the Lord Jesus Christ. We are being changed. God brings about real-time, permanent change in the lives of people like you and me.

The remarkable thing about this change process is that it takes place at the same time as something else is happening—we are getting older! Paul points that out a little later in 4 v 16: "Though outwardly we are wasting away, yet inwardly we are being renewed day by day". So physically, we are all going downhill. But spiritually? We are being changed. And this transformation is real. If you know what to look for, it is actually pretty easy to spot: it looks like holiness.

HOLINESS: WHAT CHANGE LOOKS LIKE AND WHY IT MATTERS

We tend not to use words like "holy" or "holiness" much these days. I think that's because these words do smell a bit of a pompous piety which sits smugly looking down its nose at others, feeling "holier than thou". It's also because in the past, lots of teaching about our need to be "holy" was terribly human-centred, often having the unintended effect of turning us in on our ourselves rather than outward to Jesus Christ. But that doesn't mean there is anything wrong with the concept—in fact, if we are going to live for Christ, we really need to know about holiness! Not least because it's one of the Bible's favourite words to sum up what God is like and, by extension, what he wants us to be like.

When the Old Testament says that God is holy (as in Isaiah 6 v 3: "Holy, holy, holy is the LORD Almighty; the whole earth is full of his glory"), it captures the fact that he is completely morally pure. God has never done and will never do anything wrong. He is perfectly just, fair and kind. Describing God as holy also underlines the fact that he is utterly superior to us in every way. He is infinitely smarter, more loving, more powerful and so on. So how can people like us even approach a God like this, never mind have a relationship with him? Back on Mount Sinai, the people of Israel had to keep their distance because when ordinary, unholy people got too close to the holy God, it didn't end well (people died). This God is holy—set apart in a league of his own. And it is God's holiness that provides a double-strength barrier to people like us knowing a God like him.

The great news is that when we come to the New Testament, God makes it clear that because we are in Christ, and because of what Christ is doing in us by the Spirit, holiness is no longer out of our reach. Let me unpack that a bit. There are four key things about holiness which every Christian needs to know:

First, we are holy. Because we have been united to Christ, we are "positionally" holy. God considers us to be morally pure in his sight because we are "in Christ", who is holy—his holiness is counted as ours. Now God has set us apart to be one of his people; we are "God's holy people", who are already "seated ... in the heavenly realms in Christ Jesus"

(Ephesians 1 v 1, 2 v 6). It's as if our names have been switched from the "unholy column" to the "holy column".

Second, we long to be holy. If we have been brought to life by the Spirit of holiness, then it's natural to want to be holy. In the last chapter we saw how the gospel pushes us to face what we are like. The good news is that the Spirit gives us the desire to see the "holiness gap" between ourselves and God narrowed—to be not just positionally holy but personally holy. To be a Christian is to long to be more like Christ. God's work of making us holy (sometimes called "sanctification") produces in us the same qualities that shaped Jesus' life. To be holy is to be loving, self-controlled, selfless, gentle with our words and pure in our thoughts. This is what God wants us to aim for: "Make every effort to live in peace with everyone and to be holy; without holiness no one will see the Lord" (Hebrews 12 v 14).

Third, we are becoming more holy. As we saw in 2 Corinthians 3 v 18, Paul is adamant that God is at work in us as the Spirit applies the gospel to our mind and heart and character to bring about real and lasting change: "We ... are being transformed into his image with ever-increasing glory". This is what we should expect. This is what we should pray for. This is what we should long for. This is what we should pursue. And importantly, this is what God really is doing. So when you see growing godliness in yourself and others, thank God! The gospel-shaped life is one of change, of progression, of growth in holiness. In every phase and stage of life, our great concern should be that God would use every event, every decision, every failure, every success to make us more like Christ.

Fourth, we will be holy. When the apostle John was writing about this change process, this is what he said: "Dear friends, now we are children of God, and what we will be has not yet been made known. But we know that when Christ appears, we shall be like him, for we shall see him as he is. All who have this hope in him purify themselves, just as he is pure" (1 John 3 v 2-3). John explains that we have been set apart as "children of God" through trusting in the gospel. We're still a work in progress, but one day, in eternity, we shall be "like Christ"—totally pure, holy, perfect. And how will we know that this process is complete? Because we will be able to take in the majesty and beauty of God himself. This is how it's going to end for us. I can't wait! No more having to deal with our own mixed motives, our hypocrisy, our self-deceit or our self-promotion. No more being surprised by our own capacity to be mean and our own inability to be instinctively loving. Just God-like beauty, tenderness, purity and integrity. And it's *this* hope that pushes us to strive for purity in the present.

TWO WAYS IN WHICH GOD CHANGES US

Ok, so God is committed to making people like us who are already *in* Christ *like* Christ in every way. That's a long-term project—but how does it actually happen? How do we change? And how come it often appears to be such a slow, stop-start, one-step-forward-two-steps-back process? Let's think about two ways in which God changes us: through our conscience and through our suffering.

1. THE ROLE OF THE CONSCIENCE

Our conscience is the highly sensitive internal "instrument" that convicts us of the gap between what the Bible says about how we should live and how we really are living. Conscience detects where our lives don't match what we say we believe. When God speaks, it registers on our conscience.

Or it should. The problem is that our consciences are unpredictably unreliable. We have no idea when they are going to work properly and when they aren't! I used to have a car in which the heater worked about one day in three. Sometimes, a good slap on the dashboard would bring it to life. On other days, it just refused to be resuscitated. And then for no reason it would work flawlessly for three weeks and then die again. That's what our consciences are like. That explains why sometimes, when we read the Bible or hear it explained, it is as if God is screaming in our ears, saying, *Don't you realise I'm talking about you?* and on other days it has as much impact on us as piped music in an elevator.

And there is another complicating factor. Our choices can either reduce or refine the effectiveness of our conscience. When we choose to sin, it makes it much easier to ignore the needle of our conscience the next time.

An old English writer called John Flavel wrote a book in the seventeenth century which explains this beautifully. Here he is quoting an even older guy, Bernard of Clairvaux (I know the language is a bit quaint, but stick with it—it's worth it!):

> When a man accustomed to restraint, sins grievously, it seems insupportable to him, yea he seems to descend alive into hell. In process of time it seems not insupportable, but heavy, and between insupportable and heavy there is no small descent. Next, such sinning becomes light, his conscience smites but faintly, and he regards not her rebukes. Then he is not only insensible to his guilt, but that which was bitter and displeasing has become in some degree sweet and pleasant. Now it is made a custom, and not only pleases, but pleases habitually. At length custom becomes nature; he cannot be dissuaded from it, but defends and pleads for it. (John Flavel, *Keeping the Heart*, Christian Focus, 1999, p 127)

Did you catch that? Flavel explains that when we sin the first time, it feels awful. We are plagued with guilt. But gradually the attractiveness of the sin wins out, and we overcome our guilt and shame, and do it again. The second time we don't feel so bad. As we go on, we manage to suppress any warning bells in our head. The problem is that as we suppress and silence our conscience, we damage it, making it harder for us to be godly. This is what we are up against on our journey to holiness.

What we need is for God to fix our consciences. The great news is that he is willing to do it. The writer to the Hebrews assures us: "How much more, then, will the blood of Christ, who through the eternal Spirit offered himself unblemished to God, cleanse our consciences from acts that lead to death, so that we may serve the living God!" (Hebrews 9 v 14). As God gets to work on our consciences, we need to co-operate. We need to ask God to soften our hearts and straighten out our consciences. We need to read God's word with the longing and expectation that God will work through it as the Spirit gets it under our skin.

Be honest with yourself, and ask yourself if there is something that God has been saying to you that you have simply been ignoring. Have you learned to silence your conscience, as you defy God? Is there an area where you know there is a huge gap between what you are doing and what God asks of you? If there is, now would be a great time to listen, to repent and to do what he says, asking him to recalibrate your conscience.

2. THE ROLE OF SUFFERING
Another way in which God makes us more holy is through our suffering. Now let's be honest—suffering is by definition *bad*. It's hard—really hard. And yet the Bible gives us hope in that while suffering is painful, it is not pointless. God is committed to using suffering to bring about great good in the lives of his people.

According to the Bible, there are at least three kinds of suffering in this world. Some suffering is the result of the fact that the world is sick; some is because people are sinful; and some is because Satan hates Jesus and we are caught in the crossfire. But whatever its origin, within the purposes of our God, all of this suffering is designed to make us more like Christ and to display his supremacy to us and the watching world. That's why Dietrich Bonhoeffer, a pastor who would eventually be executed by the Nazis, could write that "discipleship means allegiance to the suffering Christ, and it is therefore not at all surprising that Christians should be called on to suffer. In fact it is a joy and a token of his grace" (*The Cost of Discipleship*, SCM Press, 2015, p 45). Or, as an old Australian friend used to say to me in regular emails, "Dear Gazza, please remember they crucified the Lord Jesus; why should you expect anything better?"

Please don't get me wrong: suffering, whatever its source, is horrible. Christians aren't called to love it or to seek it out. It is evidence that the world has been damaged by sin at every level. However, once we encounter Jesus Christ—God's suffering, dying, rising and reigning King—our perspective on suffering is turned completely upside down because suffering, it turns out, is one of the most important ways (perhaps even the most important way) in which God works in our lives and in our world. God uses suffering to work the gospel deeper into our lives. The death and resurrection of Jesus is the template for all that God is doing to make us holy. Christ's one-off, unique death and resurrection becomes the pattern for the gospel-shaped life.

We started off this chapter with Paul at the end of 2 Corinthians 3. If we read on in his letter, we find him using this same death-and-resurrection model in a vivid metaphor:

But we have this [gospel] treasure in jars of clay to show that this all-surpassing power is from God and not from us. (2 Corinthians 4 v 7)

The clay jar was the ancient equivalent of a paper bag—cheap, disposable and definitely NOT built to last. That's what we're like. We are new people "in Christ", but we walk around in bodies which are rapidly wearing out. The fact that life is hard both accelerates the process of decay and makes it more and more obvious that God is at work in us:

We are hard pressed on every side, but not crushed; perplexed, but not in despair; persecuted, but not abandoned; struck down, but not destroyed.

(2 Corinthians 4 v 8-9)

What's really striking is that Paul is convinced that this isn't an unfortunate accident—this is the way God has set things up to show us and other people what matters:

We always carry around in our body the death of Jesus, so that the life of Jesus may also be revealed in our body. For we who are alive are always being given over to death for Jesus' sake, so that his life may also be revealed in our mortal body. (2 Corinthians 4 v 10-11)

In other words, God works through horror and heartbreak of every kind to make us more like Jesus.

Whether we are trying to cope with sickness, or temptation, or relational brokenness, or hatred for us because we belong to Christ, we can, in the words of James, "consider it pure joy, my brothers and sisters, whenever you face trials of many kinds, because you know that the testing of your faith produces perseverance. Let perseverance finish its work so that you may be mature and complete, not lacking anything" (James 1 v 2-4). Pain is a normal part of the Christian life—but with it there is joy too.

This is not just theoretical. It's real. My friend Dave is the life and soul of the party. He's a natural leader who struggles to sit still. But Dave also has a chronic, incurable nerve condition in his arms. He lives with burning pain from his elbows to his hands 24 hours a day. He can't shake hands, drive, pick up any of his four young kids or open doors. He can't put on his own seatbelt, turn a key, tie his shoelaces or take the top off the milk. He has to rely on his wife to put on his socks, cut his toenails and do a million other tiny things. And he is a church leader in an Arabic-speaking country whom God has been using in remarkable ways. Dave has written a book called *Kiss the Wave: Embracing God in Your Trials*. In it he writes this:

Our trials are an endless buffet table filled with opportunities for us to grow and look like Christ. As you struggle through your pain, be comforted that God is not wasting this trial but doing a good work in you through this hard time. We can have joy in our trials because God is working in our hearts. The pruning happening in your heart right now is difficult, but it is surely forming you into the image of Christ. It may feel like you are being chopped up in the storm of your life, but the divine gardener is pruning you so that you can bear more fruit in your life than you could ever ask for or imagine. (Dave Furman, *Kiss the Wave*, Crossway, 2018, p 132)

God has used Dave's suffering to produce in him a deep joy and contentment which reflects the Lord Jesus. This is the shape of the gospel-shaped life—a life in which we embrace suffering because *we know that this is how God works in us and in our world to produce eternal results*.

This is why Paul can write at the end of 2 Corinthians 4:

Therefore we do not lose heart. Though outwardly we are wasting away, yet inwardly we are being renewed day by day. For our light and momentary troubles are achieving for us an eternal glory that far outweighs them all. So we fix our eyes not on what is seen, but on what is unseen, since what is seen is temporary, but what is unseen is eternal. (2 Corinthians 4 v 16-18)

God really does change us through the gospel, as we pursue holiness—asking God to show us the "holiness gap" in our lives—and as we look for ways in which he's using all life's ups and downs to make us more like Jesus. Life with God is abundantly rich, and despite the pain that we all go through, it's marked by a gradually deepening joy as we see him at work. That's why the gospel-shaped life really is the only kind of life worth living.

But remember: a day will come when there is no more repenting to be done, there is no more unpleasant stuff to face, there is no more suffering to go through. One day the change process will be finished—not only will we get to gaze at the beauty of Christ for ever, but we will actually truly reflect that beauty.

And in the meantime? We do not lose heart!

5. LIVING TOGETHER FOR THE GOD OF THE GOSPEL

"Now you are the body of Christ, and each one of you is a part of it." (1 Corinthians 12 v 27)

I f we're going to live the Christian life, we have to live it together.

So far, we've seen how God introduces himself to us and draws us into the richness of his life through the gospel. He speaks to us about Jesus through the Bible in the power of the Spirit, exposing our sin through the gospel. God even transforms us *as individuals* through the power of the gospel.

But there is more. In fact, it would be deeply misleading to stop there because the Bible persistently makes it clear that we're called to live the Christian life *in community* with other believers. We are called to live *together* for the God of the gospel.

In the first letter he wrote to the Christians in Corinth, Paul spent quite some time hammering this home (largely because the Corinthians tended to split according to which preacher they liked best, or who was the most "spiritual", or who had most money and the biggest villa). In 1 Corinthians 12, Paul gives them an extended metaphor which captures the heart of what he is talking about. He says the church is like the *human body*.

> Just as a body, though one, has many parts, but all its many parts form one body, so it is with Christ. For we were all baptised by one Spirit so as to form one body—whether Jews or Gentiles, slave or free—and we were all given the one Spirit to drink.
>
> (1 Corinthians 12 v 12-13)

If we have all been joined to Christ by faith, then that means we have actually been joined to each other. This change is so profound that it redefines us. The fact that we are *in Christ* overrides the fact that we come from different ethnic or political or economic backgrounds— we belong to each other. The fact that we have all received the same Spirit poured out by Jesus ("we were all given the one Spirit to drink") means that we have the most important thing of all in common.

I have moved around a lot over the years. From Northern Ireland, where I grew up, to Scotland; then to England; then back to Northern Ireland; then to the Republic of Ireland and finally to Australia. But during those years, two things have stayed constant: my accent and the fact that God's people have welcomed me as family. The family bonds that God creates when he unites us to Christ by his Spirit trump everything else. If we are Christians, then wherever we go, we'll find people who share the life that God has given us in Christ. They won't necessarily be like us (and how boring would that be, anyway!), but this is a unity which outstrips everything else.

In 1 Corinthians 12, Paul maintains a beautiful balance between the fact that we are all individuals and yet that we are bound together in the deepest way possible. That means we can't ditch each other, or disrespect one another, or devalue each other:

> And so the body is not made up of one part but of many. Now if the foot should say, "Because I am not a hand, I do not belong to the body," it would not for that reason stop being part of the body. And if the ear should say, "Because I am not an eye, I do not belong to the body," it would not for that reason stop being part of the body. If the whole body were an eye, where would the sense of hearing be? If the whole body were an ear, where would the sense of smell be? But in fact God has placed the parts in the body, every one of them, just as he wanted them to be. If they were all one part, where would the body be? As it is, there are many parts, but one body. (1 Corinthians 12 v 14-19)

The marvellous implication of all this is that we really do need each other: "The eye cannot say to the hand, 'I don't need you!' And the head cannot say to the feet, 'I don't need you!'" (v 21). We really are in this together. All of us. The Christian life is a "team sport". So much so that "if one part suffers, every part suffers with it; if one part is honoured, every part rejoices with it. Now you are the body of Christ, and each one of you is a part of it" (v 26-27).

Christianity is a "we" and not an "I" religion. Of course, it is true that Christianity starts with "me" as an individual. God works in each of us to bring us to life and enable us to trust him. We come "through the door" one by one. But once we become part of the family, we enjoy all the richness of life in Christ *together*.

We laugh and cry together. We succeed and fail together. We struggle and rejoice together. We encourage one another and sometimes irritate one another—but we do it all *together*.

One of the great joys of living in Brisbane is watching test cricket at the Gabba (known as the "Gabbatoir" by English fans, as they haven't won there since 1988!). When I went to this summer's test match, I left the house alone. I had my own ticket with my name on it. But once through the gate, I spent the day with two of my friends sitting on either side of me, and other old friends whom I met at lunch, and then the 34,999 other people in the ground. It was an experience which was both individual and shared. The Christian life is precisely like that. We enter the Christian life as individuals, and then experience and live the Christian life in community.

To live a gospel-shaped life is to live together with and for the God of the gospel, which is why trying to live the Christian life without reference to the church makes as much sense as sitting alone in an empty cricket ground!

THREE TYPES OF CHURCH

So what exactly is church? We often use the word to describe a building ("the church on the corner") or a time when people get together ("I'm going to church"). But in the New Testament, it means something different. The word "church" is used in three senses. It can refer to...

1. all those who have been united to Christ by faith, spread across time and space (sometimes called the "universal church"—you could also describe it as the church already gathered around Jesus in heaven).

2. a group of connected churches spread across a region (so, for example, "the church at Corinth" was made up of a network of smaller units meeting in homes).

3. the local church in a specific location.

So Jesus says, "I will build my church, and the gates of Hades will not overcome it" (the global or universal meaning, Matthew 16 v 18). And Paul talks about both "the churches in Galatia" (regional, Galatians 1 v 2) and "the church that meets at [Aquila and Priscilla's] house" (obviously a local church, 1 Corinthians 16 v 19).

So it is in the context of the church—the local church to which you are committed, the wider "church" (group of churches of which you are part), and the universal church (which includes all the believers on the planet now and all those who have gone before)—that we live out the gospel-shaped life together to the glory of Jesus.

And what does this look like? Life in the church can be summed up by one word: love.

LIVING TO LOVE

Love is one of those things that is hard to define, and yet we all instinctively feel that we know what it is. For most of us, it's a vague mixture of warm and fuzzy feelings toward someone, and a desire to do nice things for other people. What the Bible means by love—and in particular the kind of love we are to show God and each other—is a bit more specific than that. Here's what one of Jesus' disciples, John, says about love in a letter to some churches:

Dear friends, let us love one another, for love comes from God. Everyone who loves has been born of God and knows God. Whoever does not love does not know God, because God is love. This is how God showed his love among us: he sent his one and only Son into the world that we might live through him. This is love: not that we loved God, but that he loved us and sent his Son as an atoning sacrifice for our sins. Dear friends, since God so loved us, we also ought to love one another. No one has ever seen God; but if we love one another, God lives in us and his love is made complete in us. (1 John 4 v 7-12)

This is one of the most profound passages in the whole Bible—but its message is pretty simple: God has loved us by sending Jesus to die in our place, turning aside God's wrath. So love is putting someone else first in the most dramatic, costly way possible. Real love is cross-shaped. The gospel announces that we are loved by God in Christ like this—and then calls us to love other people with the same kind of love.

In a way this brings us full circle. Because God is love (the Trinity of Father, Son and Spirit) and draws us right to the very heart of his perfect love, it becomes possible—and vital—for us to love one another. That might sound like a complete no-brainer, but sometimes we forget it. It's easy to get so caught up in "doing church", or getting our heads around the stuff in the Bible, that we forget to... er... do what it says. But being an unloving Christian is a contradiction in terms. This is why someone who claims to be a Christian but who has zero interest in other people in church—or who isn't part of a church and has no interest in joining one—has missed the point. "God is love", and so the gospel-shaped life is a life of love for the God of love and his people.

Love in the long haul is what it's all about. Love for people who are older and younger than you, richer and poorer than you, smarter and dumber than you. Love for people with whom you have everything or nothing in common, other than the fact that you are brothers and sisters in Christ. A life shaped by the gospel is, at its very core, a life of love.

HOW LOVE PLAYS OUT

"Ok, love is important," you might be thinking, "but are we any closer to seeing what love actually looks like?" Well, it's time to get specific. According to the Bible, love for each other shows in being concerned with three things.

1. ENCOURAGEMENT

Loving each other means throwing ourselves into encouraging each other. Hebrews 10 v 24-25 says this:

And let us consider how we may spur one another on towards love and good deeds, not giving up meeting together, as some are in the habit of doing, but encouraging one another—and all the more as you see the Day approaching.

Because we know what God has already done for us—and what he will do for us on "the Day" when Christ returns to "reboot" the universe—we are to invest in encouraging one another.

To encourage someone isn't just to cheer them on (although it includes that). It means to "fill them with courage"—to strengthen or equip them to keep going with Jesus. You can see that in what Paul writes to the church in Thessalonica:

For you know that we dealt with each of you as a father deals with his own children, encouraging, comforting and urging you to live lives worthy of God, who calls you into his kingdom and glory ... We sent Timothy, who is our brother and co-worker in God's service in spreading the gospel of Christ, to strengthen and encourage you in your faith. (1 Thessalonians 2 v 11-12; 3 v 2)

Paul's great goal was to say and do whatever it took to help these relatively new Christians to keep living the gospel-shaped life. And that's what we're supposed to do for each other.

When we meet—whether on Sundays or during the week, whether it's prearranged or we just bump into each other—the loving thing to do is to remind each other to "remember Jesus Christ" (2 Timothy 2 v 8). That means we'll constantly want to "speak the gospel" into each other's lives. And how do we do that? By asking how they are going in their relationship with Jesus, what God is teaching them through the Bible, what they are struggling with, or how we can pray for them. By being honest and real—talking about the challenges of living in repentance and faith, and the importance of growing in holiness, and how tough it is when we suffer—and then by reminding each other of the fact that we are in Christ!

Sometimes it's hard to do that. We get very easily distracted. We can be pretty shallow. At times, if we're honest, we'd rather talk about the football or what's been on TV. But if the gospel of Jesus Christ is what makes life worth living and is the key to living well, then isn't it unloving to do anything less than encourage each other? We need to be reminded of the gospel by other people, and they need the same. And don't miss the fact that we can encourage others just by showing up at church Sunday by Sunday and being there, even when we don't feel that we have much to say or offer!

Incidentally, this need for encouragement is why baptism and the Lord's Supper are a big deal in church. These are two very specific things which Jesus himself told us to do, which strengthen us by reminding us of what he has done for us in the gospel. When someone is added to the people of God, they are baptised with water as a powerful recognition of the fact that God works to bring us to new life in Christ. When we share bread and wine together to remember Jesus' death and resurrection, it is a tangible, "taste-able" demonstration of the gospel, which spurs us on to keep living for Christ. Different churches differ on the details (for example, how much water should be used for baptism; whether the children of believers are to be baptised; how often we should share the Lord's Supper). However, since the time of Jesus, almost every church has agreed that these two signs are a gift from God to encourage and strengthen us.

2. DISCIPLINE

We saw earlier that Paul dealt with the Thessalonians "as a father deals with his own children" (1 Thessalonians 2 v 11). And sooner or later, it's part of a father's responsibility to deal with bad behaviour. Love shows itself in discipline.

The word "discipline" probably conjures up all kinds of negative images in our minds—and some of us may have experienced terribly cruel and unloving treatment under the guise of that word. But that's not what we're talking about. The kind of discipline that the Bible talks about is firm but gentle, controlled and positive. It is *loving* discipline, which is always designed for our good.

The writer to the Hebrews describes how it is ultimately God who disciplines his children:

> God disciplines us for our good, in order that we may share in his holiness. No discipline seems pleasant at the time, but painful. Later on, however, it produces a harvest of righteousness and peace for those who have been trained by it. (Hebrews 12 v 10-11)

God loves us enough to intervene in our lives when we are getting things badly wrong—by shaping our circumstances, speaking to us through his word and pricking our consciences through the Spirit. The striking thing is that God also involves his people in this process. Jesus himself makes it very clear that the church has the responsibility to deal firmly but lovingly with people who are living in ways which contradict the gospel:

> If your brother or sister sins, go and point out their fault, just between the two of you. If they listen to you, you have won them over. But if they will not listen, take one or two others along, so that "every matter may be established by the testimony of two

or three witnesses." If they still refuse to listen, tell it to the church; and if they refuse to listen even to the church, treat them as you would a pagan or a tax collector. (Matthew 18 v 15-17)

Notice how the aim of this intervention is always to show you where you are going wrong and get you back on the right track. This "discipline" is always for your good and motivated by love. Sometimes this may simply be expressed as an arm round our shoulder and a word of "fatherly" advice. Sometimes, if we are damaging ourselves or other people (say, when someone is committing adultery), it may mean asking someone to stay away for a short period in an attempt to bring them to their senses. This latter type of discipline will be overseen by church leaders, and will be done out of a desire to protect and care for those under their responsibility. If it's not, then something has gone wrong.

To live a gospel-shaped life as part of a church community will mean gladly allowing the elders (or whatever name you have for your leaders) to act as loving fathers to you—encouraging and, where necessary, saying a hard word to you. This is what happens in a truly loving family.

3. EVANGELISM

So far we've focused on two "in-house" things—loving encouragement and discipline. But how are we to love people *outside* the church?

The most loving thing we can do for *anyone* is to share the momentous news of Jesus with them. Rico Tice is a man who has spent most of his working life telling people in central London about the Lord Jesus. In his book *Honest Evangelism*, he tells an embarrassing story about one of his housemates finding and listening to a cassette of an evangelistic talk he had given (yes, it was a long time ago!). After listening to Rico explain the message of Jesus, his friend was really angry with him. He said, "If that's what Rico believes, the fact that he's said nothing of it to me in months means he's not really my friend" (*Honest Evangelism*, TGBC, 2015, p 45). If we believe the gospel, then the most loving thing we can do is share the gospel with others.

And this is something God has given us to do together. As Paul writes to the church in Colossae, he asks them to pray for him as he tells people about Jesus where he is, and gives them encouragement as they do the same thing where they are:

> Pray for us ... that God may open a door for our message, so that we may proclaim the mystery of Christ, for which I am in chains. Pray that I may proclaim it clearly, as I should. Be wise in the way you act towards outsiders; make the most of every opportunity. Let your conversation be always full of grace, seasoned with salt, so that you may know how to answer everyone. (Colossians 4 v 3-6)

Whether we get to speak to large groups of people about Jesus or are talking to our neighbour over the garden fence, the goal is to *tell them about what the triune God has done to enable people like us to know and enjoy God for ever through the Lord Jesus Christ*. Of course, we need wisdom—to know what to say, how much to say and when to say it. And that, says Paul, includes living in a way which backs up rather than contradicts our message.

The way we treat people matters. So, as God's people, we should be concerned about social justice issues, and environmental issues, and economic issues, and every other kind of issue that affects people's lives. But we also need to remember that these things aren't evangelism. Evangelism is proclaiming a message because "faith comes from hearing the message" (Romans 10 v 17). Sooner or later, our loving goal in every relationship must be to explain the gospel. Sometimes, we will need to help people come to the point where they are able to listen (people who are going hungry, for example, do need to be fed first; homeless people need to be warm, dry and secure, and so on). But our great longing will be to bring people to the point where they are able to hear the gospel, and then to explain it to them. We must do this patiently, appropriately, lovingly, gently, courageously, repeatedly—but we must explain the gospel nonetheless.

God has done something so staggering for us that it would be wrong and unloving for us to keep it to ourselves. The gospel-shaped life, then, moves us to evangelism.

WHAT NOW?

If we belong to Christ, then we belong to his people. If we are part of *the* church of the Lord Jesus, then we really should—

in fact, we really must—be part of *a* local church. For one reason or another, that might not be easy for some people. If that's you, please ask someone for help—remember, church is a body designed to support one another, and that includes supporting those who find church difficult.

Or maybe you're eager to get involved in a church, but you're confused by the many varieties on offer. What kind of church should you pick? Find one where you're encouraged (in the true sense of the word) as the Bible is taught, where the leadership will take your holiness seriously and love you enough to challenge you, and where you'll be equipped for evangelism, as you live together as a gospel-shaped community.

Or maybe you are already part of a church, but reading this chapter has made you realise that you're not loving people there as you should. Anyone who's been around church for any length of time will be very aware of how hard it is for us to love one another, even (or sometimes especially) in church. (We'll also realise that it must be pretty hard for other people to love us most of the time!) So are you regularly asking God to help you to do what he does—to love the unlovely people, especially the ones who surround the unlovely you? Do you ask God to help your church family to love you (because they'll need all the help they can get)?

At this point, we probably all need to stop reading for a minute (or ten!) and face the fact that we are pretty unloving, and need to throw ourselves again in faith on the One who can help. The great relief is that we belong to the God who is love and who has already lavished his love on us in the Lord Jesus Christ. He's given us his Spirit to love one another as we live a gospel-shaped life together. The love of a true church community will always be both puzzling and attractive to those around us, to whom this kind of love is completely foreign. It will sometimes feel unnatural even to ourselves. But God can help us. He will equip us to encourage one another, watch out for each other, and step out together as we share the message of Christ. The gospel-shaped life is a life together marked by love.

6. LOOKING AT THE WORLD THROUGH THE GOSPEL

"And whatever you do, whether in word or deed, do it all in the name of the Lord Jesus, giving thanks to God the Father through him." (Colossians 3 v 17)

Every sentence in this book so far has been about setting you up to live faithfully and joyfully for the Lord Jesus Christ for the rest of your life in the whole of your life.

In this chapter we get to the "whole of your life" bit. How does living for Jesus affect our work, or what we eat, or how we spend our weekends, or how we use our phones, or what our relationships look like, or [insert a million and one other situations here]?

And this might be where you're sensing an issue. You may have picked up that the Bible doesn't try to answer every question that could conceivably come up in life. That was true even when it was first written. Think about it: there was no way that every issue that could have come up in, say, Philippi, could ever be tackled in the four chapters of Paul's letter to the Philippians. Given that, it's pretty obvious that in the Bible we're not always going to be able to find a fully spelled-out, step-by-step guide to handling the issues that we face in our place and time. But that doesn't mean that God has nothing to say about how to live, now that we're "in Christ". In fact, he's given us everything we need to *look at the world through the gospel*.

THE WORLD IN WHICH WE LIVE

We live at an exciting time. The pace of social, technological and scientific advances is staggering. In the West we are more connected, have more opportunities and are better educated than ever before. We are making advances in medicine that would have been unthinkable even a few years ago. We are pursuing justice for some (although by no means all) marginalised sections of society more wholeheartedly.

But the pace of change also means that sometimes, life can be confusing. Our increasing interconnectedness means that, on any subject, there is a bewildering array of voices demanding that we listen. These voices come from every conceivable perspective, from all over the world, from all kinds of cultures. At times all that they have in common is that they all claim to be "right". So how do we tell what really *is* right? How are we to negotiate a world like this?

While it's important to recognise that we face particular challenges living at this moment in history, it would be a mistake to think that we are unique, not least because the New Testament was written to Christians who were living in a world which was, in many key ways, remarkably like ours.

THE WORLD IN WHICH THEY LIVED

Being a first-century Christian in the Roman Empire was a complicated business. The earliest Christians lived in a world where there were more gods than you could shake a stick at. When it came to religion, the Roman way was to live and let live—so it was both irritating and very un-Roman to say differently, or to try to claim any sort of exclusivity. When it came to sex, it was a case of anything goes. Money and power were what really mattered, and most people craved both.

So it's not surprising that one of the great challenges of the early church was working out what it meant for people who were very much part of this world to become part of the church of the Lord Jesus Christ. How should new believers start to live a gospel-shaped life in a culture like theirs?

This is the question addressed by the apostle Paul in many of his letters in the New Testament. They were written to provide the new Christians in the churches he set up (and the others he visited or knew of) with a "from first principles" guide to living for Jesus Christ in a very messy and fragmented world. There is no clearer statement of this than Colossians 3 v 17:

> And whatever you do, whether in word or deed, do it all in the name of the Lord Jesus, giving thanks to God the Father through him.

Paul is writing to the church at Colossae (which is in modern-day Turkey). His point is very simple. Because we are "in Christ", absolutely everything we do is under his jurisdiction. Everything we do is empowered by what he has done and who we are in him. Everything we do flows from gratitude to him. Everything we do impacts his reputation, because it is done "in his name".

GOING ALL-IN

When I was at school, the standard punishment for various relatively minor misdemeanours was to write out the school rules. (I'm not sure they make students do that so much these days, but it was definitely a real pain!) For reasons I'd rather not disclose, I once had to write out "Rule 17" 100 times. As a result it is permanently imprinted in my memory: "Pupils must act, at all times, both inside and outside school, with courtesy and consideration, and in a manner which brings credit to themselves and to the school". Once we were enrolled, there could be no escape—the school laid claim to all of us. The school's reputation was in our hands! That's how Paul says we should think about being "in Christ": what God has done and is doing and will do for us controls everything. We need to align our thinking, our actions and even our opinions with God's on every subject under the sun—from work to money to technology to friendships, and everything in between. Every area of our life needs to be shaped and reshaped by the message of the gospel.

Now that's easy to say but hard to do. Let's be honest: most of us today hold thinking for ourselves as one of our most fundamental rights. *We* get to determine what's right and wrong. *We* get to choose what's right for us, and other people should respect our choices. Then suddenly, when we become a Christian, we discover that the God of the universe appears to have some very strong opinions about how we live. Sooner or later, we'll be confronted with what we suspected all along—that the Bible teaches some things which most people regard as hopelessly outdated, weird and even oppressive. The idea of living a gospel-shaped life starts to look very strange and not entirely attractive.

And the truth is, sometimes living God's way hurts. There's something painful about this basic shift from running our own lives and forming our own opinions to living with God at the centre. It's not always easy to pray as Jesus taught us to, and to say to God, "*Your* kingdom come, *your* will be done on earth as it is in heaven" (Matthew 6 v 10). Yet we're to live according to his agenda, not ours. Which is almost certainly what Jesus means when he says, "Truly I tell you, unless you change and become like little children, you will never enter the kingdom of heaven.

Therefore, whoever takes the lowly position of this child is the greatest in the kingdom of heaven" (Matthew 18 v 3-4). Children know that they don't call all the shots (or at least, they learn—and relearn—that!). Followers of Jesus have embraced a similar reality. He is in charge—we aren't. This is hard to come to terms with sometimes. We may not always like the consequences. But Jesus goes so far as to say, "Whoever wants to be my disciple must deny themselves and take up their cross and follow me" (Matthew 16 v 24). The "death" that Jesus is talking about means giving up all selfish agendas. It means living with and for him in every detail of our lives. It means living a gospel-shaped life.

Now with all that talk of "self-denial" and "dying" (even metaphorical dying), you could be forgiven for thinking that the Christian life doesn't sound like a whole lot of fun. But that's not strictly true, either—because while the Christian life sometimes costs, we'll never be left short-changed. The astonishing thing is that God only ever asks us to do what's both good for us and glorifying for him. God made us and loves us, so he knows what we need—to live in any other way than how he's told us would be like putting diesel in the tank of a petrol engine. Following the manufacturer's instructions is always the best bet. While it may sometimes look unattractive in the world's eyes, God promises that the gospel-shaped life is genuinely beautiful. And living his way will, in time, show the watching world something of the Lord Jesus.

In the Old Testament, God chose one nation, called Israel, to show what he's about. He rescued them from slavery in Egypt, and then brought them to the land of Canaan. He gave them rules to show them what the beautiful life there would look like. As they looked down into the land from the surrounding mountains, their longtime leader, Moses, said this:

Observe [God's laws] carefully, for this will show your wisdom and understanding to the nations, who will hear about all these decrees and say, "Surely this great nation is a wise and understanding people." What other nation is so great as to have their gods near them the way the LORD our God is near us whenever we pray to him? And what other nation is so great as to have such righteous decrees and laws as this body of laws I am setting before you today?

(Deuteronomy 4 v 6-8)

Many years later, Jesus himself picked up this same note and said, "I have come that they may have life, and have it to the full" (John 10 v 10). This is perhaps the single most important thing to get in this chapter. Jesus is not out to limit your life or make it less fun. He came to give you life—a life that overflows with joy, love and satisfaction, both now and for eternity. So his commands to us in the Bible are not cruel or arbitrary or limiting. He loves us. We can trust that doing what God says never involves missing out in the long term. The gospel-shaped life is the best life there is.

WHAT THIS LOOKS LIKE

Hopefully, you've got the fact that *whatever you do, whether in word or deed, do it all in the name of the Lord Jesus.* But what does that actually look like? How do we work that out? The Bible gives us multiple examples of how to think this through in the complexities of our own situation.

In Colossians 3 v 18 – 4 v 1, Paul looks at six different relationships *through the gospel*: those of wives, husbands, children, fathers, slaves and masters. He doesn't say everything that could be said about how a Christian should function in those roles. Nor is he implying that the gospel has nothing to say to mothers, brothers, sisters, friends, the self-employed and so on. Remember, this is a *real letter* written to *real people*—and Paul is writing to help them live for Jesus in the messy details of Colossian life—which, of course, will be slightly different to living for Jesus in Coventry, Canberra or Cleveland. But as Paul writes, he gives us a great template for doing our own thinking on our own issues and challenges.

So what does he say? He urges wives to stop trying to boss their husbands (3 v 18) and to trust their spouses to love them and lead them with Jesus as their model. He tells husbands, "Love your wives and do not be harsh with them" (v 19). When it comes to children, Paul tells them to "obey your parents in everything, for this pleases the Lord" (v 20). God has given parents the job of raising children, so one way we honour God is by obeying our parents when we are kids and continuing to honour them when we are adults. As for dads, they are to live out the gospel by nurturing and teaching their kids, rather than making them bitter, "or they will become discouraged" (v 21). Gospel-hearted dads won't crush their children.

Then Paul moves on to slaves. At that time, as much as 40% of the population was in some kind of economic slavery. It is worth knowing that slavery in the Roman world was very different to later chattel slavery in America and the Caribbean. Even so, it could still be terribly cruel—that's why elsewhere Paul lists slave traders alongside murderers as those whose lives are contrary to the gospel (1 Timothy 1 v 10), and he encourages slaves to gain their freedom if they can (1 Corinthians 7 v 21). That said, many slaves in the Roman world lived in their own homes and managed their own income. For these people, to be a "slave" really did mean something comparable in some senses to being an employee. Here's how Paul tells them to view their work:

Slaves, obey your earthly masters in everything; and do it, not only when their eye is on you and to curry their favour, but with sincerity of heart and reverence for the Lord. Whatever you do, work at it with all your heart, as working for the Lord, not for human masters, since you know that you will receive an inheritance from the Lord as a reward. It is the Lord Christ you are serving. Anyone who does wrong will be repaid for their wrongs, and there is no favouritism.

(Colossians 3 v 22-25)

Slaves are to see their bosses as appointed by Jesus himself, and so to work to please Christ. Because of that, they will be respectful, follow instructions and be completely wholehearted. They won't expect special favours (even if their boss is a Christian). Instead, they will work in a way which shows that they belong to Christ.

And masters? They are to work to the same standard: "Masters, provide your slaves with what is right and fair, because you know that you also have a Master in heaven" (4 v 1).

I hope you can see Paul's point here. Not all of us will be slaves or masters, or husbands or wives, but we will all find ourselves in a network of relationships, carrying a whole range of responsibilities and decisions. So how are we to live? We are to remember that "it is the Lord Christ [we] are serving". As people who have been united to him, we are to bring the gospel to bear on every part of our lives, with the help he provides. And that's something that we'll need to keep doing for the rest of our lives!

LOOKING THROUGH THE GOSPEL: A THREE-STEP GUIDE

The problem is that it's still a massive step—particularly if Christianity and the Bible are relatively new to us—to suddenly start thinking like this. How do we go about working out how we should think or act in our messy world? It can be helpful to begin by thinking through issues in terms of three different categories:

- Category 1: Does the Bible address this situation explicitly?

- Category 2: Does the Bible tackle a similar situation?

- Category 3: Does the Bible describe what it means to live for Christ in a way which has clear implications for this issue?

There are some enduring issues which the Bible tackles head on (what I've called Category 1). One example would be parenting. There are a range of passages which lay down some clear and timeless principles: parents should make every effort to teach their children about what God has done for us in Christ, and to model his grace to them (for example, Ephesians 6 v 4).

There other issues we'll face which are addressed in the Bible in terms of a situation which is broadly similar, even if the details differ (these come under Category 2). As we've seen, slaves were not exactly like employees, but because they are similar in some key elements, these passages provide a helpful roadmap for thinking about our attitude to our employer. The New Testament's teaching on our obligation to those in power would be a similar situation (Romans 13 v 1-7).

But there are also ethical challenges that we face which go unaddressed by, and in some cases were unknown to, the New Testament writers (and which often couldn't even have been anticipated just a few years ago). These fall under Category 3. So what are we meant to think about issues like assisted dying, refugees, institutional racism, cloning, transgender, artificial intelligence, abortion, or even something so basic as how to interact on social media? This is where it's important to learn how to work outwards from central principles which the Bible emphasises. After all, no one quite knows what the issues we face tomorrow or in ten years' time will be. So learning how to think about the implications of the gospel for these kind of emerging issues is a vital skill.

In the rest of this chapter, I'll take you *very briefly* through four worked examples of how this approach might look. If you want to think more deeply about any of these key areas, you'll find some resources to help you on page 117.

1. WORK

As we've already seen, the Bible does address the value of work, both explicitly (Category 1—see 2 Thessalonians 3 v 10-12) and in the context of the relationships between slaves and masters in the first century (Category 2—see Colossians 3 v 22 – 4 v 1). It makes it very clear that if you are a boss, you are to be a Christ-like boss. And if you are an employee, you are to be a Christ-like employee. If we belong to Christ, then that must be obvious when we're at work. The Bible also makes it clear that money will never be the ultimate driver for the Christian (Hebrews 13 v 5). All that and more is explicit. But that doesn't exhaust what the Bible has to say to workers. At work as everywhere else, Christians will be known for their integrity, selflessness and love, and for their unwillingness to trample over people in order to get ahead. They'll also be really hard workers (Proverbs 13 v 4). And Christians will take every opportunity—at lunch, at the water cooler, after work—to talk about the one who is everything to them: Jesus Christ (Colossians 4 v 2-6).

2. SOCIAL MEDIA

To state the obvious, the Bible doesn't have anything to say about Facebook or Instagram! Nor was there a New Testament equivalent. But it does have plenty to say about the way in which we present ourselves and interact with other people (so this is a "Category 3" issue). We are to make it our goal to please God, not people (2 Corinthians 5 v 9). Boasting is out, as is lying (2 Timothy 3 v 1-5). So our posts should be accurate and truthful. We aim to speak realistically about ourselves (particularly since we have admitted that we are sinful to the core) and to use our words to build up other people (Ephesians 4 v 29). Because our supreme goal is to honour Christ above all things, we'll think about what we post and what we like, and we won't react in the heat of the moment. We'll also do everything we can to commend the gospel to other people, even through social media.

3. SEX AND GENDER

If work is a subject about which the Bible talks regularly, and social media one which the Bible never addresses, this third area is one about which Scripture says a lot

(Category 1), but where we also need to apply the teaching of the Bible to very different presenting issues today (Category 3).

The best place to start is with Jesus himself:

> [4] "Haven't you read," [Jesus] replied, "that at the beginning the Creator 'made them male and female,' [5] and said, 'For this reason a man will leave his father and mother and be united to his wife, and the two will become one flesh'? [6] So they are no longer two, but one flesh. Therefore what God has joined together, let no one separate." (Matthew 19 v 4-6)

Jesus says that gender is not simply a social construct but a real thing which has been intentionally designed by God. Our gender is inherently linked to our bodies (v 4-5)—it's something we are, not only something we feel. Jesus also insists that marriage is between a man and woman for life—which was controversial for his first hearers too—and is an unimaginably precious gift. It is from this perspective that the Bible rules out sexual activity between those who are not married, irrespective of their genders or sexual orientation.

Of course, the Bible has more to say than this: that every person, regardless of their sexual history, needs to come to Jesus for forgiveness and *can* come to Jesus for forgiveness (1 Corinthians 6 v 9-11); that we should love all people, irrespective of their sexual preferences or behaviour (Mark 12 v 31); that sex is a great and positive gift of God for married couples (1 Corinthians 7 v 1-6); that it's possible to enjoy intimate, loving and fulfilling relationships without sex (1 Peter 1 v 22). Far from being restrictive, God's vision for human sexuality is good, positive and loving.

4. IDENTITY

The final example is one which has become more prominent in our culture in recent years (Category 3). Many people today are suffering from a real sense of dislocation (we don't know where we belong) and disorientation (we don't know who we are). A quick glance at what's trending on Netflix is more than enough to demonstrate that we identify with troubled heroes—the kind of characters who are desperately trying to find peace with themselves and others, despite the damaging influences of their parents / small-town upbringing / traumatic experiences / the pressure of their own remarkable genius. The problem is, of course, that this search for wholeness is never quite completed. Nor can it.

The New Testament teaches that the only place where we can find significance, security and satisfaction is in the Lord Jesus Christ himself. It is in Christ that we discover that we belong to God, that we are his precious sons and daughters, that we have no need to be afraid, and that we have been set free and have no need to hide (Romans 8 v 1-17). And it's all because we are in Christ.

Any attempt to find our identity elsewhere will end in disappointment or disaster. Our job or career, our physical power or appearance, our sexual orientation, our academic ability or even our personality can't ultimately carry the weight of providing us with the sense of significance we long for. Only Jesus Christ can do that.

EVERY ISSUE, EVERY SITUATION

I hope you see that we're only just scratching the surface. Some other areas where this kind of thinking needs to be worked out are marriage, family, politics, money, housing, holidays, sickness, death... I think you get the idea.

As a first step, why not choose an area that's relevant to you and try to put together your own summary of what a gospel-shaped life might look like? You could ask a Christian friend who's a bit further along in their journey to help you to think through which category the issue falls under, to read up on what the Bible says, and then to work out with you how that plays out today.

To live for Christ in our messy and challenging world is to commit to a lifetime of applying the gospel to ourselves and to our world, as we face predictable old challenges and unanticipated new ones. This isn't something we suss early in our journey and then check off the list as "done".

There are all kinds of resources which will help us to walk through the issues that I have highlighted (and lots more beyond that). There are clear, gospel-shaped answers to many of the challenges and dilemmas we face (and if we were in the same room, I would happily bore you with my take on them). But the answers themselves aren't really the main point I want you to take from this chapter. The point is that there is no part of your life about which Jesus says, *I'm not interested in that—I'll leave it to you.* There is no choice, no subject, and no opinion which the reality of being in Christ doesn't reshape and direct. The gospel-shaped life really is an "all-in" thing. God has invited and enabled us to live the beautiful life—the gospel-shaped life—with him. So don't settle for anything less: "Whatever you do, whether in word or deed, do it all in the name of the Lord Jesus, giving thanks to God the Father through him" (Colossians 3 v 17).

CONCLUSION: THE END OF THE BEGINNING

"I have fought the good fight, I have finished the race, I have kept the faith." (2 Timothy 4 v 7)

When I was a young Christian, I remember standing in front of a book table at a student event thinking to myself, "If I could ever get to the point where I had written a book about being a Christian—if I could see my name proudly displayed on the bookstall—then I'd know that I'd made it."

It's embarrassing to admit that now, but sadly it's true! Back then, I desperately wanted to get to the point where being a Christian was easy and I didn't need to put in hard yards anymore. I imagined a future where I didn't struggle with sin, where church always felt happy and comfortable, where the daily disciplines of Bible-reading and prayer took no self-discipline at all. I envisioned a version of myself who knew everything there was to know, who always sensed instinctively the right thing to do and who always chose naturally to do it.

In other words, I wanted to reach a point where I was so mature that I could "coast".

If the intervening years have taught me anything, it's that living for Jesus doesn't work like that. Instead—to borrow a phrase from the atheist philosopher Friedrich Nietzsche, of all people—the Christian life is about "a long obedience in the same direction".

As we've seen, living for the Lord Jesus isn't actually all that complicated. It's just hard. The challenge is to keep going, day after day, month after month, in the strength that God himself provides. And although I may have written a book with my name on, that challenge hasn't changed. The Christian life remains for me, as it is for you, a lifelong, day-by-day expedition with the Lord Jesus Christ himself.

In chapter 2 we heard Paul urge his protégé Timothy to "Remember Jesus Christ" (2 Timothy 2 v 8). He wanted Timothy to remember all that God had done and was doing and would do for him in the Lord Jesus—so that Timothy could enjoy the gospel-shaped life.

When he wrote those words, Paul was a man who was coming to the end of his "long obedience in the same direction". As he looked back on his life, he was able to say this:

I have fought the good fight, I have finished the race,
I have kept the faith. Now there is in store for me the
crown of righteousness, which the Lord, the righteous
Judge, will award to me on that day—and not only to
me, but also to all who have longed for his appearing.
(2 Timothy 4 v 7-8)

And that's my prayer for you—that one day you'll be able
to say the same thing. I hope that reading this book will
launch you on the gospel-shaped life, or encourage you to
keep running day after day with the Lord Jesus, enjoying
the abundant life that he died and rose to give you. The
Christian life now is a foretaste of the life we will enjoy for
ever—life with the Father, Son and Spirit in a brand new
creation which will just keep getting better. We'll never be
able to "coast" this side of the grave—but one day, when
we receive that crown, there will be no more hard yards
left. We really will have "arrived".

Until then, we fight to live the gospel-shaped life right
now, safe in the knowledge that this rich, full, challenging
life with Jesus Christ is the best life there is. It's the life
we were made for. It's the life that leads to life with God
for ever.

And that's what we both most need to know.

RECOMMENDED RESOURCES

CHAPTER 1

- *Knowing God* by J.I. Packer (Hodder & Stoughton, 2005)

- *Enjoying God* by Tim Chester (The Good Book Company, 2018)

- *None Like Him* by Jen Wilkin (Crossway, 2016)

- *Delighting in the Trinity* by Michael Reeves (IVP, 2012), published in the UK as *The Good God* (Paternoster, 2012)

CHAPTER 2

- *You Can Really Grow* by John Hindley (The Good Book Company, 2015)

- *Explore* Bible-reading notes (The Good Book Company, published quarterly)

- *A Praying Life* by Paul Miller (Navpress, 2017)

- *Pray Big* by Alistair Begg (The Good Book Company, 2019)

CHAPTER 3

- *A Passion for Holiness* by J. I. Packer (IVP, 1992)

- *Unstuck* by Tim Lane (The Good Book Company, 2019)

- *Journey Back to Joy* by Dai Hankey (10Publishing, 2017)

CHAPTER 4

On holiness:

- *The Hole in our Holiness* by Kevin DeYoung (Crossway, 2014)

On conscience:

- *Pure Joy* by Christopher Ash (IVP, 2012)

On suffering:

- *Kiss the Wave* by Dave Furman (Crossway, 2018)

- *The Scars That Have Shaped Me* by Vaneetha Rendall Risner (CreateSpace, 2016)

CHAPTER 5

- *Why Bother with Church?* by Sam Allberry (The Good Book Company, 2016)

- *How to Walk into Church* by Tony Payne (Matthias Media, 2015)

- *Honest Evangelism* by Rico Tice (The Good Book Company, 2015)

CHAPTER 6

On work:

- *The Gospel at Work* by Sebastian Traeger and Greg Gilbert (Zondervan, 2014)

On social media:

- *12 Ways Your Phone is Changing You* by Tony Reinke (Crossway, 2017)

On sex and gender:

- *Is God Anti-gay?* by Sam Allberry (The Good Book Company, 2013)

- *Transgender* by Vaughan Roberts (The Good Book Company, 2016)

- *Swipe Up* by Jason Roach (The Good Book Company, 2019)

On identity:

- *Be True to Yourself* by Matt Fuller (The Good Book Company, 2020)

- *Identity Theft* edited by Melissa Kruger (The Gospel Coalition, 2018)

MENTORING
QUESTIONS

One way of using this book is to ask another Christian who's been following Jesus a bit longer to read it too, and then meet up to talk about the chapters you've covered. You could use these questions to spark your discussions. Alternatively, you could think about these questions on your own, and chat to someone at your church about anything you're not sure about.

CHAPTER 1

- Before you read this chapter, how would you have summed up what being a Christian is all about? What about now?

- Have you thought much about the Trinity before? Is there anything that this chapter helped to make clearer? What is still not clear to you?

- Gary writes that our relationship with God is theological, personal and experiential. Which, if any, of those elements do you tend to underemphasise or overemphasise? How could you begin to correct the balance?

■ When you talk to non-Christians about Christianity, what impression do you think you're giving them? Is there anything that needs to change in the way that you do that?

CHAPTER 2

■ Gary writes that living as a Christian "isn't complicated; it's just hard". Have you found that to be true in your own experience? In what ways?

■ "Remember Jesus Christ, raised from the dead, descended from David" (2 Timothy 2 v 8). How would you use that verse to explain the gospel to someone else?

■ When and how do you read the Bible and pray? How do you find it?

■ What truths from this chapter particularly encourage you in that? Are there any practical changes that might help too?

CHAPTER 3

■ Since becoming a Christian, have you experienced the sense of exposure that Gary describes at the start of the chapter? When?

■ Why is sin described as "spiritual adultery"? Is that how you normally think of it?

- Look at the list of temptations on pages 52-54. What are the strong desires that you live with, and how do they show themselves in your life? What gospel truths will help you to battle against those desires?

- What most struck you about the description of repentance in this chapter? What would a day-by-day lifestyle of "repentance and faith" look like, do you think?

CHAPTER 4

- "Expectations are very, very important." Do you think you tend to expect too much or too little from the Christian life?

- Look at the four keys about holiness on pages 68-70. How have you seen yourself becoming more holy and longing to be holy? How does the fact that you are holy and will be holy encourage you personally?

- What has your conscience been telling you recently? Is there an area where you know there is a gap between what you are doing and what God asks of you?

- What do you think about the idea that God uses suffering to make us more holy? How have you seen that in your own life already, or in the life of a Christian you know?

CHAPTER 5

- What has your experience of church been so far? On a scale of 1-10, how important do you regard church to be? What would the Bible say, and why?

- How would you summarise the Bible's teaching on what love is?

- How could you seek to be more intentional about encouraging other Christians and sharing the gospel with non-Christians? Think of some specific people you want to commit to praying for.

- Have you ever experienced the type of "discipline" described in this chapter? In what ways did it turn out for your good?

CHAPTER 6

- "There is no choice, no subject, and no opinion which the reality of being in Christ doesn't reshape and direct." Why is being a Christian an "all-in" thing? Are there any areas of your life where you might currently be trying to hold out?

- Was there anything in this chapter that came as a surprise to you? What do you still have questions about?

- Pick an area that's relevant to you and put together your own summary of how the gospel-shaped life might look in regard to it, like the ones on pages 106-110: which category does it fall into? What does the Bible say? How would that play out today?

- "The gospel-shaped life is the best life there is." How have you found that to be true in your experience?

thegoodbook
COMPANY

BIBLICAL | RELEVANT | ACCESSIBLE

At The Good Book Company, we are dedicated to helping Christians and local churches grow. We believe that God's growth process always starts with hearing clearly what he has said to us through his timeless word—the Bible.

Ever since we opened our doors in 1991, we have been striving to produce Bible-based resources that bring glory to God. We have grown to become an international provider of user-friendly resources to the Christian community, with believers of all backgrounds and denominations using our books, Bible studies, devotionals, evangelistic resources, and DVD-based courses.

We want to equip ordinary Christians to live for Christ day by day, and churches to grow in their knowledge of God, their love for one another, and the effectiveness of their outreach.

Call us for a discussion of your needs or visit one of our local websites for more information on the resources and services we provide.

Your friends at The Good Book Company

thegoodbook.com | thegoodbook.co.uk
thegoodbook.com.au | thegoodbook.co.nz
thegoodbook.co.in